VITAL RECORDS

OF

BEDFORD,

MASSACHUSETTS,

TO THE YEAR 1850.

Southern Historical Press, Inc.
Greenville, South Carolina

This volume was reproduced
from a personal copy located in
the Publishers private library

All rights reserved. No part of this publication may be reproduced,
stored in a retrieval system, transmitted in any form, posted
on the web in any form or by any means without the
prior written permission of the publisher.

Please direct all correspondence and book orders to:
SOUTHERN HISTORICAL PRESS, Inc.
1071 Park West Blvd.
Greenville, SC 29611

Published 1903 by:
 The New England Historical & Genealogical Society
ISBN #978-1-63914-641-3
Printed in the United States of America

THE TOWN OF BEDFORD, Middlesex County, was established September 23, 1729, from parts of Billerica and Concord.

February 26, 1767, a part of Billerica was annexed to Bedford.

Population by Census: 1765 (Prov.), 457; 1776 (Prov.), 482; 1790 (U. S.), 523; 1800 (U. S.), 538; 1810 (U. S.), 592; 1820 (U. S.), 648; 1830 (U. S), 685; 1840 (U. S.), 929; 1850 (U. S.), 975; 1855 (State), 986; 1860 (U. S.), 843; 1865 (State), 820; 1870 (U. S.), 849; 1875 (State), 900; 1880 (U. S), 931; 1885 (State), 930; 1890 (U. S), 1092; 1895 (State), 1169; 1900 (U. S.), 1208.

EXPLANATIONS.

1. WHEN places other than Bedford and Massachusetts are named in the original records, they are given in the printed copy.

2. In all records the original spelling is followed.

3. The various spellings of a name should be examined, as items about the same family or individual might be found under different spellings.

4. Marriages are printed under the names of both parties, but the full information concerning each party is only given in the entry under his or her name. Prior to 1850, there are no records of intentions of marriage found in Bedford.

5. Additional information which does not appear in the original text of an item, i.e., any explanation, query, inference, or difference shown in other entries of the record, is bracketed. Parentheses are used only when they occur in the original text, or to separate clauses found there — such as the birth-place of parents, in late marriage records.

6. The records are printed from a copy made, and legally attested, by the Town Clerk of Bedford.

ABBREVIATIONS.

a. — age
abt. — about
b. — born
ch. — child
chn. — children
Co. — county
C.R. — church record (First Parish)
d. — daughter; died; day
Dea. — deacon
dup. — duplicate entry
G.R. — gravestone record
h. — husband
hrs. — hours.
inf. — infant
Jr. — junior
m. — married; month
min. — minutes.
M.R. — Middlesex County record (East Cambridge)
prob. — probably
rec. — recorded
s. — son
Sr. — senior
w. — wife; week
wid. — widow
widr. — widower
y. — year
1*st.* — first
2*d.* — second
3*d.* — third

BEDFORD BIRTHS.

BEDFORD BIRTHS.

To the year 1850.

ABBOT (see Abbott), Benj[ami]n, s. Moses Jr. and Allise, Jan. 11, 1794.
Betsey, d. Moses and Allis, Feb. 25, 1790.
Edward Stearns, s. Moses Jr. and Allice, Feb. 5, 1797.
Eliza, d. Moses Jr. and Allice, Dec. 10, 1801.
Lucy Stearns, d. Moses and Allyse, Feb. 11, 1792.
Moses, s. Moses Jr. and Alice, Aug. 16, 1795.
Oliver Reed, s. Moses Jr. and Allice, Mar. 26, 1800.

ABBOTT (see Abbot), Allis, d. Moses (Abbot) and Allis, Sept. 22, 1788.
Anna Lexera, d. Moses and Susan, May 24, 1834.
Bettey, d. Moses and Mary, July 12, 1757.
Charles, s. Nathaniel and Abi, Feb. 16, 1824.
Charles Edwin, s. Moses and Susan, Feb. 24, 1824.
Elizabth [dup. Elizabeth], d. Obed and Elizabth, Mar. 16, 1731.
Harvey, s. Moses Jr. and Allis, Mar. 24, 1787.
Jeremiah, s. Moses and Mary, Feb. 9, 1766.
John, s. Obed and Elizabeth, Feb. 4, 1732–3.
John, s. Moses and Mary, May 29, 1759.
John Henry, s. Moses and Susan, Aug. 16, 1825.
Mary, d. Obed (Aboot) and Elizabeth, Feb. 16, 1734–5.
Mary, d. Moses and Mary, July 2, 1768.
Moses [dup. Abboot], s. Obed and Elizabeth [dup. Abbed (Abott) and Elizabeth (Abbott Abboott)], Jan. 13, 1727 [dup. 1727–8].
Moses, s. Moses and Mary, Sept. 21, 1761.
Moses Gorden, s. Moses and Susan, June 5, 1822.
Sarah [dup. Abboott], d. Obed and Elizabeth, Apr. 22, 1729.
Susan Caroline, d. Moses and Susan, Oct. 8, 1820.
Sylvester Kinsman, s. Moses and Susan, Dec. 9, 1831.
———, ch. Moses Jr. and Allice, Dec. 5, 1798.

ADAMS, George Bryant, s. Dr. Abel B. and Mary F., July 16, 1843.
Polley, d. Joseph and Elizebeth, May 4, 1794.

ARTES, Elizabeth, "a child takin by James Willson to bring up," Feb. 7, 1747–8.

BACON, Abigail, d. Samuel and Eunice, Mar. 15, 1754.
Abigail, d. Jonathan and Abigail, Feb. 6, 1807.
Abjah, s. John and Elizabeth, Jan. 22, 1755.
Albert, s. Thompson and Martha, Aug. 24, 1802.
Albert Thompson, s. Albert and Susan, Dec. 8, 1827.
Alice, d. John O. and Clara A., Sept. 27, 1846.
Alonzo Reuben, s. Reuben Jr. and Ruth, May 4, 1834.
Ann Eliza, d. Reuben and Sarah, Sept. 3, 1821.
Anna, d. Thomas and Elizabeth, Jan 27 [blotted], 1752.
Benjamin, s. Benjamin and Katharine, July 6, 1741.
Benjamin, s. Benjamin and Esther, May 6, 1769.
Benjamin, s. Benjamin Jr. and Martha, Jan. 13, 1801.
Caroline, d. Jonathan and Abigail, July 25, 1813.
Catherine, d. Benjamin Jr. and Martha, Mar. 27, 1816.
Charles, s. Flag and Patte, May 18, 1792, in Lexington.
Clara Estelle, d. Edward and Charlotte (b. Wethersfield, Vt.), June 2, 1849.
Clark, s. Jonathan and Abigail, Sept. 15, 1808.
David, s. Josiah and Sarah, Aug. 30, 1730.
David, s. Michael and Elizabeth, June 2, 1752.
Ebenezer, s. Josiah and Sarah, Sept. 15, 1736.
Edward, s. John and Betsey, Feb. 15, 1817.
Elbridge, s. Thompson and Martha, Aug. 2, 1800.
Elijah, s. Benj[amin] and Catharine, Sept. 19, 1754.
Eliza, d. Thompson and Martha, Oct. 4, 1799.
Eliza Ann, d. Jonathan and Abigail, Apr. 13, 1818.
Elizabeth, d. John and Elizabeth, Sept. 25, 1745.
Elizabeth, d. Thomas and Elizabeth, Feb. 26, 1749–50.
Elizabeth, d. John and Elizabeth, June 25, 1750.
Elizbeth, d. Abijah and Rhoda, Aug. 29, 1776.
Elizeboth, d. Mical and Elezeboth, Nov. 19, 1747.
Ellen A., d. Isaac P. and Susan E., Sept. 27, 1835.
Emely Frances, d. Edward and Charlotte, May 27, 1843.
Emma Augusta, d. Jonathan and Abigail, Dec. 15, 1831.
Esther, d. Benj[ami]n Jr. and Esther, Mar. 24, 1767.
Esther Davis, d. Benjamin Jr. and Martha, July 24, 1795.
Flagg, s. David and Lucretiea, Apr. 9, 1771.
Fredrick, s. Jonathan and Abigail, July 13, 1811.
Hannah, d. John and Hannah, Dec. 11, 1779.
Helen Frances Adaline, d. Reuben and Sarah, Apr. 25, 1830.
Henry Augustus, s. John and Betsey, Aug. 16, 1838.

BACON, Isaac, s. Benjamin and Catharine, May 6, 1748.
Isaac, s. Benjamin and Catharine, Oct. 27, 1751.
Isaac, s. Benjamin and Esther, Apr. 24, 1773.
Isaac Preston, s. Benjamin Jr. and Martha, July 13, 1807.
Izza, d. Oliver and Sarah, Apr. 25, 1779.
James, s. Josiah and Sarah, June 30, 1738.
Jeremiah, s. Benjamin and Martha, Dec. 9, 1809.
Jerome Augustus, s. Jonathan and Abigail, June 21, 1827.
Jesse, s. John and Elizabeth, Aug. 2, 1749.
Jesse, s. Benjamin and Esther, July 6, 1775.
Job Lane, s. Benj[am]i[n] Jr. and Martha, July 17, 1804.
John, s. John and Elizabeth, Dec. 24, 1746.
John, s. John and Elizabeth, Mar. 22, 1753.
John, s. Thompson and Martha, Dec. 22, 1786.
John Otis, s. John and Betsey, Sept. 1, 1822.
Jonas, s. Thomas and Elizabeth, May 8, 1764.
Jonathan, s. Thompson and Martha, Apr. 15, 1785.
Joseph, s. Josiah and Sarah, Mar. 24, 1745.
Joseph, s. Samuel and Eunice, Nov. 18, 1751.
Joshua, s. Josiah and Sarah, Sept. 14, 1732.
Joshua, s. Samuel and Eunice, Feb. 23, 1760.
Katharine, d. Benjamin and Esther, Mar. 4, 1771.
Kathrine, d. Benjamin and Kathrine, July 9, 1746.
Liday, d. Josiah and Sarah, Aug. 23, 1747.
Lucy, d. Oliver and Sarah, Sept. 28, 1781.
Lydia, d. Thomas and Elizabeth, Oct. 5, 1769.
Lydia Ella, d. Edward and Charlotte, June 14, 1845.
Maria Louisa, d. Elbridge and Louisa, Apr. 4, 1824.
Martha, d. Michael and Elizabeth, June 27, 1762.
Martha, d. Reuben and Sarah, Mar. 22, 1814.
Martha Sylvania, d. Benjamin 3d and Sylvania, July 31, 1822.
Mary, d. Josiah and Sarah, Feb. 5, 1742.
Mary, d. Samuel and Eunice, Dec. 31, 1765.
Mary Jane, d. Reuben and Sarah, Mar. 14, 1824.
Molly, d. Michael and Elizabeth, Jan. 6, 1758.
Nabbe, d. Oliver and Sarah, Nov. 4, 1773.
Nancy, d. Thompson and Martha, Jan. 19, 1793.
Nancy, d. Reuben and Sarah, Oct. 22, 1809.
Nathan, s. Mical and Sarah, Sept. 10, 1744.
Nathan, s. Michael and Elizabeth, Mar. 24, 1754.
Nathan, s. David and Lucretiea, Aug. 17, 1772.
Noah, s. Samuel and Eunice, Jan. 26, 1756.
Octa, s. Thompson and Martha, Feb. 27, 1795.
Oliver, s. Oliver and Sarah, July 12, 1776.

BACON, Orlando, s. Reuben Jr. and Ruth, Feb. 6, 1836.
Polla, d. Oliver and Sarah, Aug. 4, 1787.
Rebekah, d. Samuel and Eunice, Feb. 11, 1764.
Reuben, s. John and Elizabeth, Feb. 4, 1758.
Reuben, s. Thompson and Martha, Feb. 17, 1784.
Reuben, s. Thompson and Martha, Nov. 25, 1788.
Reuben, s. Reuben and Sarah, Dec. 8, 1811.
Reuben Alonzo, s. Reuben Jr. and Ruth, July 1, 1838.
Rhoda, d. Benj[amin] and Catharine, Oct. 30, 1757.
Rhoda, d. Thomas and Elizabeth, Nov. 19, 1758.
Salle, d. Oliver and Sarah, Sept. 1, 1771, in Medford.
Samuel, s. Samuel and Eunice, Feb. 16, 1749–50.
Sarah, d. Joseph and Rebeca, Jan. 30, 1730–1.
Sarah, d. Josiah and Sarah, Aug. 18, —— [rec. between June 30, 1738, and Feb. 5, 1742].
Sarah, d. Michal and Elizabeth, Feb. 17, 1749–50.
Sarah, d. Benjamin Jr. and Martha, Mar. 2, 1794.
Sarah, d. Benjamin and Martha, Jan. 5, 1803.
Sarah, d. Reuben and Sarah, May 19, 1807.
Seth, s. Samuel and Eunice, Sept. 26, 1761.
Simon, s. David and Lucretia, Mar. 20, 1779.
Solomen, s. Michael and Elizabeth, Mar. 8, 1756.
Stephen, s. Samuel and Eunice, Mar. 24, 1758.
Stephen, s. Benjamin and Esther, Sept. 28, 1778.
Susanna, d. Michael and Elizabeth, Mar. 27, 1760.
Susanna, d. Michael and Elizabeth, Jan. 8, 1765.
Sylvester, s. Benj[ami]n Jr. and Martha, Jan. 13, 1809.
Thompson, s. John and Elizabeth, Mar. 5, 1760.
Thompson, s. Thompson [and] Martha, Apr. 16, 1797.
Walter Franklin, s. Warren and Lucy, Mar. 9, 1846.
Warren, s. Jonathan and Abigail, Jan. 13, 1816.
Warren, s. Jonathan and Abigail, Nov. 30, 1822.
Wiliam, s. Jonathan Jr. and Ruth, Nov. 5, 1730.
Wiliam, s. Josiah and Sarah, Aug. 8, 1734.
William, s. David and Lucretia, Apr. 12, 1774.
William, s. David and Lucretia, Nov. 22, 1775.
William F., s. Isaac P. and Susan E., Feb. 10, 1834.

BALL, Briggs, s. Jonathan and Abiel, July 5, 1790.
John, s. Jonathan and Abiel, July 1, 1783.
Jonathan, s. Jonathan and Abiel, May 13, 1787, in Lexington.
Salle, d. Jonathan and Abiel, June 23, 1781.

BALLARD, Benjamin, s. Dr. Joseph and Sarah, Jan. 7, 1770.

BALLARD, Joseph, s. Dr. Joseph and Sarah, Feb. 3, 1772.
Sarah, d. Dr. Joseph and Sarah, Jan. 26, 1774.

BANCROFT, Elizabeth, d. William and Elizabeth, Dec. 16, 1744.
William, s. W[illia]m and Elizabeth, June 19, 1743.

BARRETT, Frederick, s. William and Helen A., Mar. 1, 1848.

BIGELOW, Winslow, s. Charles and Rebecca, June 16, 1846.

BLANCHARD, Caroline A., d. Isaac and Caroline, July 8, 1842, in Charlestown.

BLODGETT, Ordillers Motes [?], s. Simeon and Sally, Sept. 17, 1805.

BLOOD, Abraham, s. Jeremiah and Sarah, Oct. 26, 1776.
Daniel Hartwell, s. Jeremiah and Sarah, Aug. 20, 1765.
Francis Hartwell, s. Jeremiah and Sarah, Aug. 5, 1769.
Hannah, d. Jeremiah and Sarah, Aug. 31, 1771, in Lincoln.
Israel Meeds, s. Jeremiah and Sarah, Aug. 17, 1763.
Jeremiah, s. Jeremiah and Sarah, Sept. 13, 1767.
Sarah Barras, d. Sarah, Jan. 15, 1761.
Solomon, s. Jeremiah and Sarah, Sept. 23, 1773.
————, d. Amariah and Elizabeth, May 14, 1846.

BOWERS, Bradley, s. Bradley and Martha, Dec. 16, 1821.
Bradley Virnum, s. Bradley and Lydia, Feb. 20, 1796.
John M., s. Bradley and Martha, July 19, 1819.
Lydia Moore, d. Bradley and Lydia, July 3, 1799.

BOWES, Dorkis, d. Rev. Nicholas and Lucy, Aug. 15, 1744.
Elizabeth, d. Rev. Nicholas [and] Lucy, Feb. 23, 1739–40.
Lucy, d. Rev. Nicholas and Lucy, June 20, 1736.
Lydia, d. Rev. Nicholas and Lucy, Dec. 17, 1749.
Mary, d. [Rev.] Nicholas and Lucy, Feb. 22, 1755.
Nicholas, s. Rev. Nicholas and Lucy, Oct. 20, 1737.
Thomas, s. Rev. Nicholas and Lucy, June 18, 1747.
William, s. Rev. Nicholas and Lucy, Dec. 3, 1734.

BOWMAN, Abel, s. Abel and Lucy, Dec. 14, 1787, in Billerica.
Abel, s. Jonas and Abigail, Feb. 12, 17[ ].
Abigail, d. Abel and Lucy, Apr. 22, 1778.
Easter, d. Nathan and Easter, June 19, 1774.
Ebenezer, s. Jonas and Abigail, Mar. 17, ———.
Francis, s. Abel and Lucy, Mar. 12, 1783.

BOWMAN, Hannah, d. Francis and Sarah, Nov. 10, 1760.
Hannah, d. Jonas and Abigail, Nov. 4, 17[ ].
Jane, d. Ebenezer and Rosanna, May 1, 1784.
John, s. Ebenezer and Rosanna, Jan. 5, 1782.
John, s. Abel and Lucy, Mar. 10, 1790, in Billerica.
Jonas, s. Jonas and Abigail, Dec. 16, 17[ ].
Joseph, s. Jonas and Abigail, Sept. 19, 17[ ].
Lucy, d. Abel and Lucy, Jan. 5, 1777.
Lydia, d. Abel and Lucy, Aug. 16, 1792, in Billerica.
Nathan, s. Nathan and Easter, Apr. 2, 1772.
Polley, d. Abel and Lucy, Dec. 17, 1779.
Rosanna, d. Ebenezer and Rosanna, Nov. 5, 1779.
Ruth, d. Nathan and Easter, Aug. 29, 1776.
Ruth, d. Jonas and Abigail, Feb. 5, 17[ ].
Ruthe, d. Abel and Lucy, Mar. 4, 1786.
Sarah, d. Francis and Sarah, Apr. 14, 1757.

BROOKS, Edwin Marcellus, s. Silas and w., Sept. 14, 1843.
Frank Alden, s. Silas (b. Worcester) and Nancy (b. Marlborough), Dec. 1, 1849.

BROWN, Abigail, d. Nathaniel and Ruth, Mar. 19, 1803.
Abram English, s. Moses and Elizabeth (b. Boston), Jan. 21, 1849.
Alden, s. Moses and Elizabeth, Sept. 12, 1846.
Alden T., s. Elijah and Mary, Dec. 18 [1847].
Anna, d. Nathaniel and Ruth, Mar. 23, 1799.
Hannah, d. Joseph and Desire, Feb. 15, 1761.
John, s. Nathaniel and Ruth, Sept. 19, 1800.
John Henry, s. Moses and Elizabeth, Sept. 26 [1844].
John Page, s. Nathaniel and Ruth, Jan. 12, 1810.
Joseph, s. Joseph and Rachell, Apr. 27, 1820.
Joseph Winthrop, s. Joseph and Sarah, Dec. 8, 1845.
Mary Ann, d. Nathaniel and Ruth, Sept. 6, 1805.
Moses Fitch, s. Joseph and Rachel, Apr. 13, 1823.
Ruth Davis, d. Nathaniel and Ruth, Oct. 11, 1807.
Submit, d. Joseph and Desire, Jan. 31, 1763.

BRYANT, Ellen Louisa, d. Nathaniel and Mary, Mar. 6, 1846.
Sarah Amelia, d. Nathan and Mary, June 24, 1843.

BUTLER, Elanor Maria, d. Samuel and Mary, Sept. 14, 1843.
Harriat Adeline, d. Samuel and Mary, Aug. 13, 1836.

BUTTERFIELD, Charles Herbert, s. Sidney (b. Lexington) and Julia Ann (b. Lexington), Jan. 6, 1849.
Eldora, d. John and w., May 29, 1843.

BUTTERFIELD, Ellen Elizabeth, d. Joseph M. and Clarissa, Jan. 23, 1837.
Ellen Maria, d. Joseph M. and Clarissa, Sept. 22, 1839.
Matilda, d. Charles and w., Mar. 18, 1844.

BUTTERS, Daniel Henry, s. Daniel and Susan, June 17, 1819.
George Andrew, s. Daniel and Mary, Apr. 16, 1847.
Rebekah, d. Franklin and Rebekah, Nov. 22, 1820.
Thomas Goodwin, s. Daniel and Susan, Jan. 6, 1821.
William Henry, s. Daniel and Mary, Sept. 21, 1843.
———, s. Daniel and Mary, June 7, 1845.

BUTTRICK, Elisabeth, d. Willard and Mary, Oct. 6, 1810.
Esther, d. Willard and Mary, Oct. 14, 1808.
Harriet, d. Willard and Mary, Mar. 31, 1816.
John Proctor, s. Willard and Mary, May 6, 1804.
Mary Ann, d. Willard and Mary, Apr. 23, 1806.
Samuel Bartlett (Butrick), s. Willard and Mary, Oct. 16, 1801.
Sarah Catherine, d. Willard and Mary, Apr. 19, 1818.
Sarah Catherine, d. Willard and Lucy, May 24, 1843.
Susanna Eleanor, d. Willard and Mary, Dec. 2, 1813.
Willard, s. Willard and Mary, July 14, 1822.

CALDWELL, Adam, s. Adam and Phebe, July 7, 1754.
Edith, d. William and Edith, Jan. 24, 1782, in Cambridge.
Joseph Porter, s. William and Edith, Feb. 10, 1783.
William, s. Adam and Phebe, June 4, 1760.
William, s. William and Edith, Nov. 22, 1781.

CAREY (see Cary), John Francis, s. Matthew and Mary, Mar. 16, 1845.

CARY (see Carey), James, s. James and Rebacah, June 11, 1732.
Rebecah, d. James and Rebeccah, July 14, 1735.

CENTRE, ———, s. Rodney and w., Feb. 13, 1844.

CHAMBERLAIN (see Chamberlin), Almira, d. Phinehas W. and Almira, Apr. 3, 1834.
Benjamin Adams, s. Phineas Esq. and Dorcas, June 22, 1806.
David Varnum, s. Phineas and Dorcas, Mar. 6, 1801.
Dorcas, d. Phinehas and Dorcas, Dec. 6, 1797.
Enoch Lane, s. Phineas and Dorcas, Feb. 8, 1808.
Henry, s. Phinehas W. and Esther, Oct. 12 [1844].
Lydia Smith, d. Phinehas and Dorcas, Oct. 25, 1799.
Phineas Whitney, s. Phineas Esq. and Dorcas, Sept. 3, 1803.

CHAMBERLAIN, Phinehas, s. Phineas W. and Esther, Apr. 5, 1847.
Phinehas, s. Phinehas and Esther (b. Concord), Sept. 3, 1848.
———, ch. P. W. and Esther, Aug. 28, 1843.

CHAMBERLIN (see Chamberlain), ———, ch. Phin[ea]s, Feb. 22, 1805. c.r.

CHAMBERS, James, s. James and Margerit, Jan. 15, 1742.

CHEEVER, Daniel, s. Israel and Bridget, June 28, 1693.

CLARK, Alice, d. Leander and Laura, Sept. 3, 1845.
Ellen, d. James and Hannah, Apr. 29, 1821.
Elmira, d. James and Hannah, July 20, 1832.
Elsey, d. James and Hannah, Aug. 23, 1819.
Marshall, s. James and Hannah, Mar. 10, 1823.
Samuel, s. William and Sarah, Nov. 24, 1843.
Shirley Sumner, s. James and Hannah, Sept. 13, 1827.

COLBURN, Eliza Caroline, d. Jonas W. and Elizabeth, Nov. 20, 1825.
Leonard Hoar, s. Jonas W. and Elizabeth, June 6, 1828.

COLMAN, Joseph Allen, s. Eben (b. Ashby) and Emma H. (b. Groton), June 1, 1848.

COMEY, William, s. William and Elmira, Mar. 4, 1846.

CONVASS (see Convers), Bettey, d. Joseph and Elizabeth, Mar. 7, 1763.
James, s. Joseph and Elizabeth, Feb. 26, 1772.
John, s. Joseph and Elizabeth, Apr. 19, 1783.
Joseph, s. Joseph and Elizabeth, Jan. 26, 1765.
Josiah, s. Joseph and Elizabeth, May 10, 1769.
Molley, d. Joseph and Elizabeth, July 13, 1777.
Sarah, d. Joseph and Elizabeth, May 4, 1767.
Thaddeus, s. Joseph and Elizabeth, Feb. 4, 1779.
William, s. Joseph and Elizabeth, Oct. 12, 1774.

CONVERS (see Convass), Eliza French, d. William (Convars) and Sarah, Oct. 10, 1801.
Joshua, s. Joseph (Convass) and Elizabeth, Aug. 19, 1786.
Sally, d. William and Sarah, Apr. 12, 1804.
Sarah, d. William and Sarah, Apr. 12, 1803.

COOPER, Willie Nelson, s. William H. (b. Littleton) and Rachel, Nov. 14, 1848.

CORBIT, William, s. John and Sari, May 15, 1746.

COTTING, Charles Henry, s. John R. and Sarah C., Apr. 20, 1841.
James Albert, s. James S. and Susannah, Nov. 24, 1841.

CROSBY, Alice Maria, d. Cyrus and Louis, Nov. 5, 1846.
Artemas, s. Dea. Michael and Asenath, Nov. 27, 1806.
Aseanath, d. Dea. Michael and Aseaneth, Jan. 6, 1794, in Andover.
Asenath, "2d Daughter of that name," d. Dea. Michael and Asenath, Apr. 23, 1812.
Ellen Lucretia, d. Cyrus F. and Lois, Nov. 4, 1844.
Franklin, s. Dea. Michael and Asenath, Sept. 22, 1808.
Frederick, s. Dea. Michael and Aseanath, Sept. 2, 1795, in Andover.
Frederick, s. George and w., Dec. 11, 1842.
George, s. Dea. Michael and Asenath, Mar. 6, 1805.
George, s. George and w., Mar. 3, 1838.
Loammi, s. Dea. Michael and Aseanath, Oct. 2, 1801, in Littleton.
Louisa, d. Dea. Michael and Asenath, June 18, 1803, in Littleton.
Mary, d. Dea. Michael and Aseanath, June 19, 1799, in Andover.
Mary Louisa, d. George and Louisa, Aug. 5, 1848, in Burlington.
Michael, s. Dea. Michael and Aseaneth, Apr. 29, 1792, in Billerica.
Michael, s. George and w., Jan. 9, 1833.
Rachel, d. Dea. Michail and Aseaneth, July 15, 1797, in Andover.
Theadore Wallace, s. Cyrus F. (b. Billerica) and Lois, Dec. 19, 1848.
William, s. George and w., July 6, 1840.

CROWLEY, Jeremiah, s. Michael and Mary, Oct. 9, 1843.

CUTLER, Albert, s. Thomas C. and Maria W., July 8, 1829.
Clarke Cooledge, s. Thomas C. and Lois W., July 7, 1841.
Emerson Bartlett, s. Amos B. and Mary P., June 14, 1836.
Frederic Amos, s. Amos B. and Mary P., Aug. 17, 1840.
George, s. Thomas C. and Maria W., Feb. 8, 1834.
George, s. James and w., Aug. 28, 1843.
Grace Ann Elizette, d. Nathaniel C. and Susan G., June 1, 1844.
Leonard, s. Thomas C. and Maria W., Sept. 10, 1836.

CUTLER, Lois Maria, d. Thomas C. and Lois, Mar. 12, 1845.
Mary Susan Adelaide, d. Amos B. and Mary, July 25, 1846.

CUTTING, Mary Louisa, d. John R. (b. Charlestown) and Evaline H. (b. Marblehead), Apr. 11, 1849.

DANDLY (see Danley), William, s. Cornelius, May 29, 1750.

DANFORTH, Benjamin, s. Benj[amin] and Sarah, Mar. 11, 1755.
Dolley, d. Benja[min] and Sarah, Oct. 11, 1751.
Sarah, d. Benjamin and Sarah, June 18, 1749.

DANLEY (see Dandly), Mary, d. Cornalos and Lilly, May 27, 1746.

DAVES (see Davis), John, s. Stephen and Elizabeth, July 29, 1737.

DAVIS (see Daves), Abby Caroline, d. Eleazer P. and Susan, Sept. 14, 1846.
Abigail, d. Eleazer and Rebekah, Aug. 8, 1774.
Abigal, d. Eleazer and Rebakah, Oct. 23, 1741.
Adron, s. Stephen and Elizabeth, Apr. 24, 1727.
Allice Amelia, d. Simon and Alice, Feb. 14, 1812.
Ambrose Abbott, s. Simon and Allise, Nov. 21, 1809.
Amos, s. Daniel and Mary, Apr. 8, 1711.
Amos, s. Amos and Rebakah, Sept. 19, 1742.
Benjamin Josiah, s. Eleazer Jr. and Martha, Dec. 20, 1810.
Bethi, d. Sam[ue]l and Olive, Jan. 27, 1774.
Betsey, d. Thaddeus and Sarah, Dec. 30, 1783.
Betsey, d. Eleazer Jr. and Martha, Dec. 26, 1799.
Bettey, d. Eleazer and Rebekah, Feb. 16, 1765.
Danil, s. Daniel and Mary, Sept. 19, 1701.
Danil, s. Josiah and Elizabeth, Apr. 3, 1742.
Dolle, [twin] d. Samuel and Olive, May 12, 1781.
Dorcas, d. Stephen and Eliz[abet]h, Oct. 21, 1758.
Ebenezer, s. Stephen and Elizabeth, July 6, 1751.
Eleazer, s. Eleazer and Rebekah, Jan. 13, 1768.
Eleazer Page, s. Eleazer Jr. and Martha, Jan. 30, 1805.
Elezabeth, d. Stephen and Elizabeth, Mar. 12, 1743-4.
Elezar, s. Elezar and Rebecah, May 30, 1734.
Elizabet, d. Eleazar and Rebakah, July 2, 1739.
Elizabeth, d. Stephen and Elizabeth, Jan. 11, 1714.
Elizabeth, d. Josiah and Elizabeth, Feb. 19, 1743-4.
Ellen Amelia, d. Eleazer P. and Susam M., Mar. 10, 1845.

DAVIS, Ephraim, s. Daniel and Mary, Jan. 27, 1706.
Ephraim, s. Ephraim and Rebakah, Mar. 11, 1740-1.
Ester, d. Stephen and Elizabeth, May 28, 1746.
Ezra, s. Daniel and Mary, Aug. 14, 1721.
Frederic, s. Thaddeus H. and Almira, Mar. 28, 1845.
Frederick, s. Thaddeus H. and Almira, Mar. 28, 1846.
George, s. Eleazer and Martha, Sept. 8, 1819.
Hannah, d. Ephraim and Rebakah, Aug. 6, 1739.
Hannah, d. Stephen and Elizabeth, Oct. 17, 1748.
Hannah, d. Josiah and Elizabeth, Oct. 13, 1755.
Hannah, d. Stephen and Elizabeth, June 5, 1761.
Hannah, d. Eleazer and Rebekah, Aug. 26, 1771.
Hannah Skinner, d. Eleazer Jr. and Martha, May 25, 1813.
Harvey Gardner, s. Simon and Allise, June 24, 1808.
Isaac Stearns, s. Dea. Thaddeus and Sarah, Nov. 20, 1794.
Isaac Stearns, s. Job and Mary, Apr. 26, 1807.
Joanna, twin d. Eleazer and Rebekah, Aug. 19, 1769.
John, s. Stephen Jr. and Lydia, June 7, 1769.
John Skinner, s. Eleazer Jr. and Martha, May 6, 1801.
John Urvine [?], s. Job and Mary, Feb. 3, 1811.
Jonas, s. Stephen and Elizabeth, Sept. 4, 1723.
Jonathan, s. Danil and Mary, Feb. 15, 1700.
Jonathan, s. Josiah and Elizabeth, May 23, 1748.
Joseph, s. Timothy and Hannah, Feb. 20, 1739-40.
Josiah, s. Daniel and Mary, July 9, 1713.
Josiah, s. Josiah and Elizabeth, Nov. 11, 1737.
Kathrine, d. Nathanel and Susana, Nov. 20 [? 12], 1747.
Lucy, d. Eleazer and Rebekah, July 11, 1766.
Lucy Emeline, d. Simon and Allise, Apr. 8, 1807.
Lydia [dup. Lida Daves], d. Stephen and Elizabeth, July 25, 1730.
Lydia, d. Stephen and Elizabeth, Apr. 17, 1756.
Marcy, d. Daniel and Mary, Nov. 18, 1703.
Marcy, d. Daniel and Mary, July 23, 1725.
Martha Joanna, d. Eleazer Jr. and Martha, Oct. 5, 1808.
Martha Maria, d. Eleazer Jr. and Martha, Sept. 10, 1817.
Mary, d. Daniel and Mary, Apr. 4, 1719.
Mary, d. Josiah and Elizabeth, Mar. 6, 1739-40.
Mary, d. Eleazer and Mary, Aug. 19, 1760.
Mary, d. Eleazer Jr. and Martha, Mar. 22, 1803.
Mary, d. Simon and Allice, Aug. 17, 1813.
Mary Louisa, d. Thaddeus H. and Almira, Feb. 18, 1848.
Molley, d. Stephen Jr. and Lydia, Sept. 18, 1767.
Nancy, d. Dea. Thaddeus and Sarah, May 28, 1791.

DAVIS, Nathan, s. Daniel and Mary, Mar. 31, 1708.
Nathaniel, s. Daniel and Mary, Nov. 3, 1715.
Olive, d. Samuel and Olive, Sept. 8, 1772.
Orpha Pultania, d. Job and Mary, May 4, 1809.
Paul, s. Josiah and Elizabeth, Jan. 8, 1745–6.
Paul, s. Samuel and Olive, Mar. 14, 1779.
Phillip, s. Stephen and Elizabeth, May 17, 1719.
Phillip Jr., s. Stephen and Elizabeth, Apr. 7, 1721.
Polley, d. Dea. Thaddeus and Sarah, Apr. 2, 1789.
Rebecah, d. Elezar and Rebecah, Aug. 2, 1736.
Rebekah, d. Eleazar and Mary, June 18, 1762.
Ruth, d. Stephen and Elizabeth, Aug. 24, 1724.
Ruth, d. Stephen and Elizabeth, Dec. 5, 1739.
Sally, d. Thaddeus and Sarah, July 2, 1780.
Samuel, s. Stephen and Elizabeth, Mar. 22, 1729.
Samuel, s. Eleazar and Rebakah, Aug. 21, 1747.
Samuel, s. Josiah and Elizabeth, Apr. 20, 1750.
Samuel, s. Samuel and Olive, Sept. 4, 1776.
Samuel, s. Eleazer Jr. and Martha, Aug. 15, 1815.
Samuel Gilson, s. Thaddeus Jr. and Sally, Feb. 17, 1808.
Samuel Warren, s. T. Horatio and Almira S., Sept. 9, 1843.
Sarah, d. Eleazer and Rebakah, Oct. 13, 1743.
Sarah, twin d. Eleazer and Rebekah, Aug. 19, 1769.
Stephen, s. Stephen and Elizabeth, Nov. 6, 1715.
Stephen, s. Stephen and Elizabeth, Nov. 27, 1741.
Stephen, s. Thaddeus and Sarah, July 30, 1787.
Sukey, d. Dea. Thad[deu]s and Sarah, Sept. 18, 1795.
Susanna, d. Daniel and Susanna, Nov. 6, 1767.
Susanna, d. Eleazer Jr. and Martha, Jan. 7, 1807.
Tabitha, d. Stephen and Elizabeth, Sept. 12, 1717.
Tabitha, d. Josiah and Elizabeth, May 12, 1753.
Thaddeus, s. Stephen and Elizabeth, Feb. 5, 1754.
Thaddeus, s. Thaddeus and Sarah, Jan. 3, 1782.
Thaddeus Horatio, s. Thaddeus Jr. and Sally, Mar. 8, 1808.
Timothy, s. Timothy and Hannah, May 16, 1738.
Warren, s. Thaddeus Jr. and Sally, May 5, 1810.
[torn]hraim, [twin] s. Samuel and Olive, May 12, 1781.

DEAN, Elizabeth, d. Thaddeus and Elizabeth, Aug. 30, 1779.
Ezra, s. Thaddeus and Susanna, Mar. 1, 1794.
Fanna, d. Thad[deu]s and Susanna, July 7, 1788.
James, twin s. Thaddeus and Elizabeth, Apr. 1, 1781.
Nance, d. Thad[deu]s and Susanna, Dec. 12, 1786.
Nancy, d. Thaddeus and Susanna, Nov. 4, 1790.

DEAN, Phinaas, twin s. Thaddeus and Elizabeth, Apr. 1, 1781.
Rhoda, d. Thad[deu]s and Susanna, Mar. 17, 1798.
Supply, d. Thaddus and Susanna, Apr. 27, 1796.
Susana, d. Thaddeus and Elizabeth, Mar. 11, 1783.
Thaddeus, s. Thaddeus and Elizabeth, Feb. 25, 1778.
Thaddeus, s. Thaddeus and Susanna, Aug. 2, 1792.

DEXTER, Lois, d. Nathan and Phebe, Mar. 8, 1782.
Nathan, s. Nathan and Phebe, May 15, 1777.
Susanna, d. Nathan and Phebe, Aug. 19, 1779.

DINSMOOR (see Dinsmor), Abraham, s. Thomas and Hannah, Feb. 22, 1729-30.
Susanah, d. Thomas and Hannah, July 8, 1727.

DINSMOR (see Dinsmoor), Abel, s. Thomas and Hannah, Sept. 27, 1736.
Elifilet, s. Thomas and Hannah, Dec. 23, 1734.
Hannah, d. Thomas and Hannah (Dinsmoor), Dec. 22, 1725.
John, s. Thomas and Hannah, Jan. 24, 1732-3.
Thomas, s. Thomas and Hannah, Mar. 5, 1730-1.

DIX, Frederick, s. Jonathan and Abigail, Mar. 18, 1800.
Susen, d. Jonathan and Abigail, Jan. 23, 1802.

DRURY, Garsham, s. Zedediah and Hannah, Dec. 31, 1739.
Zedekiah, s. Zedekiah and Hannah, Mar. 1, 1741 [*sic*, see death rec. of Hannah].

DUDLEY, Hannah Lavina, d. Silas and Hannah, Sept. 26, 1827.
Silas, s. Silas and Hannah, June 11, 1823.
Stillman, s. Silas and Hannah, Nov. 20, 1825.

DUREN, Abraham, s. Jonos and Ester, July 15, 1778.
Anna, d. Jonos and Easter, Oct. 9, 1781.
Asa, s. Reuben and Mary, May 11, 1778.
Elnathan, s. Reuben and Mary, Oct. 8, 1786.
Joel, s. Reuben and Mary, June 22, 1780.
Joseph, s. Reuben and Mary, July 30, 1784.
Nathaniel Gould, s. Reuben and Mary, Nov. 26, 1781.
Reuben, s. Reuben and Mary, Aug. 14, 1775.

DUTTEN (see Dutton), Hannah, d. Samuel and Martha, Apr 21, 1745.
Pattee, d. Samuel and Martha, Apr. 10, 1742.
Samuel, s. Samuel and Martha, July 11, 1743.
Seth, s. Samuel and Martha, Apr. 9, 1747.

BEDFORD BIRTHS.

DUTTON (see Dutten), Albert Lee, s. Hiram L. and Ellen, Nov. 24, 1844.
Ellen Frances, d. Hiram and Ellen, Apr. 20, 1847.
Emeline, d. Hiram (b. Greenfield, N.H.) and Ellen (b. Andover), Dec. 4, 1848.
Excy Maria, d. George and Lydia P., Oct. 13, 1832.
George Henry, s. Hiram L. and Ellen, Mar. 25, 1846.
Hannah, d. David and Hannah, May 25, 1773.
Katherine, d. David and Hannah, Nov. 9, 1762.
Louisa Caroline, d. George and Lydia P., Nov. 22, 1841.
Lucy Abigail, d. George and Lydia P., Sept. 28, 1843.
Lydia Ann, d. George and Lydia P., Oct. 29, 1829.
Mary Jane, d. George and Lydia P., June 1, 1831.
Nathaniel, s. David and Hannah, Sept. 1, 1766.
Pamelia Estelle, d. George and Lydia P., Dec. 23, 1846.
Sarah, d. David and Hannah, Sept. 8, 1761.

EDWARDS, Emma L., d. Robert W. and Emeline, May 8, 1846.
Rachel Ann, d. Robert and Emaline (b. Sudbury), Feb. 25, 1849.
William Augustus, s. William and Emeline, May 12, 1844, in Scituate.

ELIOT, Bettee, d. Joseph and Mary, May 27, 1753.

EMERY, Francis Wolcott Reed 3d, s. S. Hopkins and Julia R., Apr. 24, 1842.

EVERETT, William, s. William and Anna, June 10, 1828.
William Dickson, s. William and Eliza A., Apr. 15, 1832.

FARLE, Johanah, d. Benjmin and Johanah, Apr. 22, 1733.

FARMER, Ann Augusta, d. Peter and Dorcas, Nov. 16, 1834.
Hiram Augustus, s. Peter and Dorcas, Jan. 1, 1828.

FASSET, Amos, s. John and Mary, June 13, 1752.
Amos, s. Asa and Margaret, Mar. 10, 1783.
Asa, s. Josiah and Joanna, Feb. 27, 1752 " new stile."
Benjamin, s. Asa and Margaret, Sept. 7, 1787, in Sherburn.
David, s. John and Mary, Apr. 29, 1747.
Joann, d. Josiah and Joanna, Jan. 24, 1758.
John, s. John and Mary, June 23, 1743.
Jonathan, s. John and Mary, Apr. 26, 1745.
Josiah, s. Josiah and Joanna, Mar. 25, 1750.
Josiah, s. Asa and Margaret, Aug. 26, 1778.
Nathan, s. John and Mary, Apr. 2, 1749.

FASSET, Sarah, d. John and Mary, May 18, 1742.
Sarah, d. Josiah and Joanna, Sept. 22, 1755.
Susanna, d. Josiah and Jomna [Joanna], Mar. 24, 1747–8.
Timothy, s. Asa and Margaret, Feb. 23, 1781.

FISK (see Fiske), David, s. Robert and Elizabeth, Feb. 16, 1748–9.
George Nourse, s. George and Arinda, May 12, 1825.
Jonathan Lane, s. George and Arinda, Oct. 8, 1834.
Nathan Lord, s. George and Arinda, Oct. 9, 1826.
Sarah Maria, d. George and Arinda, Nov. 28, 1832.

FISKE (see Fisk), Anne Eliza, d. George and Arinda, Aug. 27, 1830.
David Abbott, s. George (Fisk) and Arinda, July 30, 1828.

FITCH, Abel, s. David Jr. and Olive, Apr. 25, 1809.
Abel Porter, s. Abel and Nancy, Sept. 17, 1837.
Albert, s. Almond and Martha, Feb. 14, 1817.
Alford, s. Jeremiah and Lydia, Apr. 8, 1771.
Alford, s. Jeremiah and Lydia, Aug. 2, 1786.
Allis, d. Zech[ariah] and Eliz[abet]h, Nov. 10, 1759.
Almen, [twin] s. Jeremiah Jr. and Lydia, Aug. 8, 1780.
Amos, s. Jeremiah Jr. and Lydia, July 26, 1782.
Benjamen, s. Benjamin and Meriam, Jan. 6, 1736–7.
Benjamin, s. Nathan and Louisa, Sept. 30, 1838.
Daniel, s. Zech[a]r[iah] and Eliz[abet]h, Feb. 21, 1764.
David, s. Benjamin a[nd] Meriam, May 22, 1743.
David, s. David and Mary, June 28, 1777.
David, s. David Jr. and Hannah, Feb. 20, 1802.
Delia Adalaide, d. Joel and Susanna, May 17, 1840.
Ebenezer, s. Zacheriah and Elizabeth, Sept. 4, 1743.
Ebenezer, s. Zech[a]r[iah] and Eliz[abe]th, Aug. 5, 1751.
Elijah, s. Moses and Rachel, Jan. 10, 1790.
Elizabeth, d. Jeremiah and Elizebeth, Dec. 24, 1738.
Elizabeth, d. Zacheriah and Elizabeth, Jan. 6, 1738–9.
Elizabeth, d. Jeremiah and Elizabeth, Aug. 7, 1752.
Ella, d. Albert and Almira (b. Burlington), Jan. 16, 1849.
Ellen Maria, d. Albert and Elmira, Sept. 2, 1846.
Ester, d. Zacheriah and Elizabeth, Sept. 12, 1745.
Esther, d. Zech[a]r[iah] and Eliz[abe]th, Oct. 13, 1749.
Eunice, d. Benja[min] and Miriam, July 26, 1747.
Hannah, d. Benjamin and Meriam, June 10, 1733.
Hannah Procter, d. David Jr. and Hannah, Dec. 10, 1803.
Harvey William, s. Mary, May 8, 1798.

FITCH, Isaac, s. Benjamin and Meriam, May 18, 1752.
Isaac, s. David and Mary, Jan. 15, 1782.
Isaac, twin ch. David and Olive, Dec. 23, 1824.
Isaac Emerson, s. Nathan and Louisa, Nov. 30, 1836.
Jeremiah, s. Jeremiah and Elizabeth, Sept. 25, 1742.
Jeremiah, s. Jeremiah and Lydia, May 14, 1778.
Joanna, d. Jeremiah and Elizabeth, Feb. 29, 1747-8.
Joel, s. Moses and Rachel, June 12, 1794.
John, [twin] s. Jeremiah and Elizabeth, Aug. 14, 1745.
John, s. Jeremiah and Lydia, Feb. 6, 1785.
John Moses, s. Moses Jr. and Polley, July 8, 1811.
Jonas, s. Zacheriah and Elizabeth, Feb. 5, 1740-1.
Jonathan Simonds, s. David and Olive, Mar. 15, 1815.
Joseph, s. Joseph and Sarah, July 14, 1734.
Joseph, s. Joseph and Sarah, Oct. 2, 1746.
Joseph, s. Thaddeus and Mary, July 10, 1797.
Lowes, d. Ben[j]a[min] and Meriam, Oct. 31, 1740.
Lucy, d. Zech[a]r[iah] and Eliz[abet]h, July 22, 1747.
Lucy, d. Zech[a]r[iah] and Eliz[abe]th, July 6, 1753.
Lucy, d. Moses and Rachel, July 17, 1785.
Lucy, twin ch. David and Olive, Dec. 23, 1824.
Lydia, d. Benjamin and Meriam, Mar. 21, 1745.
Lydia, d. David and Mary, Dec. 7, 1772.
Lydia, d. Jeremiah and Lydia, Jan. 17, 1773.
Lydia, d. Jeremiah and Lydia, Sept. 6, 1774.
Lydia [twin ch. Jeremiah Jr. and Lydia], Aug. 8, 1780.
Lydia S., d. Almond and Martha, May 14, 1815.
Marshal, s. Nathan and Loisa, Dec. 16 [1844].
Martha Simonds, d. David and Olive, May 29, 1817.
Mary, d. Thaddeus and Mary, Dec. 29, 1779.
Mary Fowle, d. David Jr. and Olive, Feb. 11, 1806.
Mary Fowle, d. David Jr. and Olive, May 29, 1807.
Mathew, [twin] s. Jeremiah and Elizabeth, Aug. 14, 1745.
Meriam, d. Benjamin and Meriam, Jan. 23, 1734-5.
Moley, d. Joseph and Sarah, Oct. 16, 1737.
Moses, s. Jeremiah and Elizabeth, Mar. 3, 1755.
Moses, s. Moses and Rachel, Mar. 28, 1787.
Moses Josiah, s. Joel and Susanna, Aug. 24, 1834.
Nancy Jane, d. Abel and Nancy, Aug. 16, 1836.
Nathan, s. Benja[min] and Miriam, Jan. 27, 1748-9.
Nathan, s. Moses and Rachel, Oct. 22, 1797.
Nathan, s. David Jr. and Olive, Feb. 13, 1811.
Nathan, s. Capt. Joel and Susanna, May 25, 1822.
Nathan Andrew, s. Nathan and Louisa B., Sept. 9, 1835.

FITCH, Olive, d. David and Olive, Apr. 24, 1820.
Olive Maria, d. Nathan and Louisa (b. Bolton), Oct. 1, 1849.
Patta, d. Jeremiah and Elizabeth, July 14, 1750.
Phebe, d. Zech[a]r[iah] and Eliz[abe]th, Nov. 25, 1756.
Polly, d. David and Mary, Oct. 23, 1770.
Rachel, d. Moses and Rachel, Nov. 30, 1791.
Rachel Ann, d. Joel and Susanna, Aug. 14, 1829.
Rebekah, d. Zech[ariah] Jr. and Rebekah, July 4, 1759.
Sally Reed, d. Alford and Sally, Feb. 19, 1820.
Samuel, s. Jeremiah and Elizabth, Nov. 9, 1736.
Sarah, d. Joseph and Sarah, Mar. 25, 1732.
Sarah, d. Zech[a]r[iah] and Eliz[abe]th, Jan. 2, 1755.
Sarah, d. Thaddeus and Mary, Sept. 22, 1781.
Silas, s. Nathan and Louisa, Aug 1, 1840.
Solomon, s. Moses and Rachel, Nov. 8, 1783.
Susanna, d. Joseph and Sarah, July 22, 1743.
Susanna, d. Capt. Joel and Susanna, Mar. 5, 1820.
Susanna, d. Capt. Joel and Susanna, Aug. 13, 1825.
Susanna, d. Capt. Joel aud Susanna, Feb. 8, 1827.
Thaddeus, s. Capt. Joseph and Rachel, Mar. 23, 1755.
William, s. Zachriah and Elizabeth, Feb. 19, 1735-6.
Zachriah, s. Zachriah and Elizabth, Apr. 1, 1734.
———, d. Nathan and Louisa, Oct. —, 1846.

FLINT, Sarah Caroline, d. Edward and Sarah, Mar. 16, 1833.
———, ch. Abel and Susan B., May 9, 1846.

FOSTER, Abner, s. Noah and Grace, Feb. 6, 1800.

FOWLE, Jonathan Lawrence, s. Samuel and Rachel, Mar. 10, 1797.
Joseph, s. Samuel and Rachel, Feb. 20, 1793.
Polly, d. Samuel and Rachel, Oct. 24, 1788.
Samuel, s. Samuel and Rachel, May 23, 1791.

FRENCH, Abigail, d. Rev. Samuel of Andover, w. Rev. Samuel Stearns, May 29, 1776. G.R.

FROST, George Henry, s. William F. and Rebecca, Nov. 1, 1843.
Gideon Frothingham, s. Frederick A. and w., May 29, 1848.
Lucy J., d. William F. (b. Billerica) and Rebecca (b. Ashby), May 26, 1848.
William, s. William and Rebecca, Oct. 6, 1845.

GLEASON (see Gleson), Alfred Waldo, s. Lewis P. and Lucy, Aug. 12, 1842.

BEDFORD BIRTHS.

GLEASON, Alpheas, s. Charles and Abigail, Mar. 17, 1820.
Benjamin, s. Joel and Lydia, May 20, 1820.
Caroline, d. Lewis P. and Sophronia, Jan. 3, 1827.
Caroline Maria, d. Lewis P. and Lucy, June 10, 1832.
Charles, s. Jonas and Abigail, Mar. 14, 1798.
Charles Edwin, s. Lewis P. and Lucy, Apr. 18, 1830.
Charles Lemuel, s. Charles and Abigail, Jan. 23, 1823.
Dorcas, d. Jonas and Ruth, Aug. 13, 1786.
Elizabeth Frances, [twin] d. Lewis P. and Lucy, May 23, 1835.
Henry Augustus, s. Lewis P. and Lucy, Jan. 6, 1829.
Jeremiah, s. Jonas and Abigail, Feb. 10, 1796.
John Francis, [twin] s. Lewis P. and Lucy, May 23, 1835.
Jonas, s. Jonas and Ruth, Feb. 12, 1780.
Lewis Putnam Jr., s. Lewis P. and Lucy, Aug. 16, 1837.
Lewis Putnam Jr., s. Lewis P. and Lucy, June 1, 1839.
Lucy Caroline, d. Lewis P. and Lucy, Sept. 9, 1846.
Lucy Stone, d. Joel and Lydia, May 16, 1823.
Lydia, d. Joel and Lydia, Mar. 27, 1816.
Simean, s. Jonas and Ruth, July 15, 1782.
Sophia Maarh, d. Charles and Abigail, Jan. 3, 1828.
Susannah, d. Joel and Lydia, Feb. 3, 1812.

GLESON (see Gleason), Hannah, d. Jonas and Ruth, Sept. 17, 1775.
Rhoda, d. Jonas and Ruth, Sept. 28, 1777.

GOLDEN, Charles W., s. Edward and w., Apr. 17, 1849.

GOODELL, Amos, s. Amos and Ema, July 2, 1763.
Elizabeth, d. Amos and Ema, Aug. 1, 1767.

GOODRIDGE (see Goodritch), Francis Bowman, s. Capt. William and Hannah, June 29, 1800.

GOODRITCH (see Goodridge), Charlotte, d. Capt. William and Hannah, July 25, 1795.
Sophia, d. Capt. William and Hannah, Dec. 26, 1793.

GOODWIN, Ann, d. Uriah and w., Dec. 10, 1803.
Charles Wellington, s. Henry and Sarah E., Sept. 4, 1843.
Henry Oliver, s. Henry and Sarah Elizabeth, June 25, 1839.
Herbert Nelson, s. William (b. Boston) and Eliza J. (b. Burlington), Oct. 15, 1849.
Joseph Augustus, s. Henry and Sarah, Oct. 31, 1845.
Mary, d. Uriah and w., June 26, 1791.
Sally, d. Uriah and w., June 7, 1800.

GOODWIN, Stephen, s. Uriah and w., Apr. 17, 1806.
Susan, d. Uriah and w., Aug. 18, 1796.
Thomas, s. Uriah and w., Aug. 5, 1798.
Timothy, s. Uriah and w., Aug. 3, 1793.
Uriah, s. Uriah and w., June 9, 1789, in Billerica.
William Wallace, s. William and Eliza, Feb. 28, 1846.
———, s. Henry and Sarah, Apr. 13, 1847.

GRAGG, Caroline Eliot, d. Charles and Eliot, Sept. 25, 1822.
Charles, s. Charles and Eliot, Feb. 7, 1826.
Charles Cornelius, s. Charles and Eliot, Feb. 2, 1827.
Edward, s. Charles O. and Elliott, Oct. 11, 1847.
Emily Cordelia, d. Charles O. and Eliot, May 31, 1833.
Harriet A., d. Charles O. and Eliot, Nov. 22, 1845.
Helen Maria, d. Charles O. and Eliot, May 29, 1831.
Lucy Augusta, d. Charles and Eliot, June 20, 1824.
Mary Josephine, d. Charles O. and Eliot, Aug. 24, 1838.
Mary Josephine, d. Charles O. and Eliot, June 29, 1842.
Sarah Alice, d. Charles O. and Eliot, Oct. 22, 1828.
William Henry, s. Charles O. and Eliot, Oct. 12, 1843, "this should be 1835."

GREEN, Abel Gilman, s. Abel and Nabby, Nov. 24, 1820.
Leonard Franklin, s. Abel and Nabby, Mar. 2, 1833.
Mary Abigail, d. Abel and Nabby, Sept. 6, 1825.
Perly, s. Abel and Nabby, Apr. 18, 1823.

GRIMES, Elizabeth, d. Jonathan and Janes, Sept. 7, 1747.

GROVER, Abigal, d. Thomas and Abigal, Nov. 30, 1729.
John, s. Thomas and Abigal, Dec. 5, 1727.
Thomas, s. Thomas and Abigal, Mar. 25, 1725.

HADLEY, Andrew, s. Simon and Olive, Nov. 15, 1797.
Israel Porter, s. Simon and Olive, May 1, 1796.
Joseph Porter, s. Simon and Olive, Sept. 22, 1791.
Lydia, d. Simon and Olive, Nov. 15, 1801.
Olive, d. Simon and Olive, Nov. 4, 1799.
Polly, d. Simon and Olive, Oct. 27, 1794.
Sewall, s. Simon and Olive, Dec. 2, 1792.

HAPGOOD, Ellen Frances, d. Cyrus (b. Acton) and Ellen (b. Acton), Aug. 24, 1849.

HARRINGTON (see Herington, Herrington), Jonathan, s. Henery and Sarah, Mar. 6, 1744–5.

HARTWEL (see Hartwell, Heartwel, Heartwell), Danel, s. Danel and Sarah, Mar. 14, 1734–5.
Joseph, s. William and Deborah, Nov. 3, 1730.
Sarah, d. Danel and Sarah, Oct. 4, 1736.
Wiliam, s. Wiliam (Hartwell) and Debrah, June 9, 1733.

HARTWELL (see Hartwel, Heartwel, Heartwell), Abby Louisa, d. Amos and Louisa, June 15, 1839.
Abigail, d. Solomon and Abigail, Apr. 11, 1760.
Amos Edward, s. Amos and Louisa, Sept. 23, 1828.
Benjamin Franklin, s. Joseph and Hannah (b. Carlisle), Jan. 25, 1848.
Caroline Augusta, d. Joseph 2d and Hannah, Apr. 19, 1841.
Charles Henry, s. Joseph 2d and Hannah, Oct. 5, 1836.
Daniel, s. Solomon and Abigail, Apr. 5, 1762.
Dolle, d. Joseph and Jemima, Jan. 10, 1764.
Edwin Augustus [dup. omits Augustus], s. Eldridge and Lucy P. [dup. omits P.], Sept. 12, 1845.
Ellen Elizabeth French [dup. omits French], d. Joseph [dup. 2d] and Elizabeth [dup. Hannah], May 28, 1843.
Ellen Francena, d. Joseph 2d and Hannah, July 18, 1839.
Frederick Alonzo, s. Amos and Louisa, June 13, 1841.
George, s. Timothy Jr. and Lucy, Mar. 17, 1791.
George [ch. William and Mary], Aug. 4, 1814.
George Alfred, s. Joseph and w. [dup. Hannah], Dec. 7, 1845 [dup. 1844].
Hannah, d. Joseph and Jemima, July 9, 1759.
Hannah Elizabeth, [twin] d. Joseph 2d and Hannah Hodgman, May 13, 1835.
Harriet Frances, d. Joseph and Elizabeth, Apr. 28, 1846.
Isaac, s. William and Joanna, Mar. 1, 1804.
James, s. William and Deborah, June 1, 1739.
Jemima, d. Joseph and Jemima, Sept. 6, 1753.
John, s. Joseph and Jemima, May 18, 1755.
John Bachelder, s. William and Joanna, June 27, 1808.
Joseph, s. Joseph and Jemima, May 13, 1752.
Joseph, s. Joseph and Jemima, May 9, 1762.
Joseph, s. Joseph and Elizabeth, May 26, 1806.
Joseph Edwin, [twin] s. Joseph 2d and Hannah Hodgman, May 13, 1835.
Liza [ch. William and Mary], Dec. 31, 1811.
Lucy, d. Benjamin F. and Lucy, May 19, 1830.
Lydia, d. Joseph and Jemima, Nov. 1, 1757.
Martha Jane, d. Joseph and Elizabeth, Jan. 25, 1842.

HARTWELL, Mary, d. Amos and Louisa, Mar. 19, 1825.
Mary Ann, d. Joseph and Naomi S. [dup. omits S.], Apr. 18, 1832.
Mary Joanna, d. William and Joanna, May 17, 1806.
Molley, d. Joseph and Jemima, Apr. 5, 1769.
Nancy Jane, d. Joseph 2d and Hannah, Jan. 3, 1838.
Oliver, s. William and Deborah, Jan. 30, 1727-8.
Ruth, d. Joseph and Jemima, Feb. 2, 1761.
Salle, d. Stephen Jr. and Sarah, May 5, 1780.
Samuel, s. Stephen and Rebekah, Feb. 8, 1756.
Samuel Chandler, s. William and Mary, Feb. 4, 1810.
Sarah, d. Dea. Amos and Louisa, Feb. 28, 1827.
Sarah Joanna, d. Amos and Louisa, Aug. 31, 1823.
Solomon, s. Danel and Sarah, Apr. 20, 1739.
Timothy, s. Joseph and Jemima, Sept. 7, 1765.
William, s. Joseph and Jemima, June 25, 1770.
William Green, s. Amos and Louisa, Dec. 1, 1834.
―――, d. Timothy and Mary, Mar. 28, 1753.
―――, s. Joseph and Hannah, Nov. 28, 1846.

HASTENS (see Hastings), Jason, s. William and Ruth, Jan. 2, 1743-4.
William, s. William a[nd] Ruth, Jan. 26, 1741-2.

HASTINGS (see Hastens), Francis, s. Justus P. (b. Swansey, N.H.) and Maria L. (b. Boston), Oct. 9, 1848.
Jacob G., s. Justus P. and Maria L., Jan. 21, 1844.

HAYWARD, Ann Maria, d. Moses and Lucretia, Sept. 11, 1831.
Caroline, d. Mather and Lucy, July 31, 1813.
Charlotte Lucretia, d. Moses and Lucretia B., June 8, 1830.
Ebenezer, s. Mather and Lucy, Oct. 1, 1802.
Ebenezer Henry, s. Ebenezer and Esther, Nov. 4, 1829.
Esther Maria, d. Eben[eze]r and Esther, Nov. 5, 1831.
George Bingham, s. Ebenezer and Ann T., Aug. 3, 1844.
Hannah Elvira, d. Ebenezer and Sarah, Mar. 26, 1818.
Harriet Francis, d. John and Lydia, May 12, 1831.
John Augustus, s. John W. and Lydia H., Mar. 14, 1828.
John White, s. Mather and Lucy, July 11, 1804.
Lucy Ann, d. Mather and Lucy, Aug. 8, 1809.
Maria, d. Mather and Lucy, Nov. 1, 1819.
Mather, s. Mather and Lucy, Apr. 12, 1811.
Moses, s. Mather and Lucy, Dec. 30, 1800.

HAYWARD, Stephen Lane, s. John W. and Lydia H., Oct. 26, 1829.
William Page, s. Mather and Lucy, Dec. 2, 1807.

HEARTWEL (see Hartwel, Hartwell, Heartwell), Abigal, d. Stephen and Mary, Aug. 15, 1744.
Elizabeth, d. Daniel (Heartwe[l]) and Sarah, Oct. 20, 1745.
Mary, d. Stephen (Heartwell) and Mary, Dec. 19, 1742.
Ruth, d. Stephen and Mary, Mar. 1, "175 new stile."
Ruth, d. Willlam and Deborah, Jan 17, ———.
Stephen, s. Stephen and Mary, Oct. 12, 1749.
Tabitha, d. Stephen and Mary, Nov. 24, 1746.
William, s. Daniel and Sarah, Sept. 1, 1743.

HEARTWELL (see Hartwel, Hartwell, Heartwel), Amos, s. William and Joanna, Aug. 3, 1798.
Benjamin Farley, s. William and Joanna, June 8, 1800.
Joseph, s. William and Joanna, Apr. 7, 1802.
Stephen, s. Stephen and Sarah, May 18, 1785.
William, s. William and Joanna, Jan. 12, 1797.
———, d. Timothy and Mary, June 4, 1750.

HENEREY (see Hennry), James, s. Hugh and Mary, Mar. 24, 1732.
John, s. Hugh and Mary, Aug. 13, 1730.

HENNRY (see Henerey), Elizabeth, d. Hugh (Henry) and Mary, Aug. 7, 1734.
Esther, d. Hugh and Mary, May 23, 1736.
Margrat, ch. H[u]gh and Mary, Feb. 8, 1727, "before Bedford was a Town."
Mary, ch. H[u]gh and Mary, Feb. 4, 1723, "before Bedford was a Town."

HERINGTON (see Harrington, Herrington), Jeremiah, s. Henery and Sarah, Apr. 19, 1742.
John, s. Henery and Sarah, Feb. 29 [sic], 1739.

HERRINGTON (see Harrington, Herington), Thomas, s. Henery and Sarah, May 12, 1747.

HILL, Artemas, s. Josiah and Susanna, Oct. 3, 1809.
Constantine, s. Josiah and Susanna, May 18, 1812.
Elijah Bacon, s. Josiah and Susanna, Apr. 24, 1795.
George, s. Constantine and Martha P., Feb. 10, 1846.
Joseph, s. Josiah and Susanna, Feb. 23, 1793.

HILL, Josiah, s. Josiah and Susanna, July 11, 1791.
Josiah, s. Joseph and Susan, Feb. 28, 1817.
Lucy, d. Josiah and Susanna, Dec. 11, 1800.
Lucy, d. Josiah and Susanna, July 27, 1802.
Mary, d. Jonathan and Abigal, July 27, 1734.
Mary Elizabeth, d. David and Lydia P., July 21, 1847.
Susanna, d. Josiah and Susanna, Apr. 30, 1798.

HOAR, Maria Adeline, d. Edward and Betsey, Jan. 3, 1846.

HODGMAN, Amanda Jane, d. Joseph B. and Caroline M., Nov. 10, 1844.
Charles Otis, s. Joseph B. and Mary, Aug. 27, 1835.
John Franklin, s. Joseph B. and Mary, Mar. 1, 1834.

HOSMER, Angeline, d. Leander and Sophronia, Apr. 1, 1820.
Ann M., d. L[eander] and S[ophronia], Sept. 2, 1821.
Anna Fosgate, d. Castalio and Ruth, Mar. 28, 1808.
Caroline M., d. Leander and Sophronia, Jan. 6, 1825.
Castalio, s. Castalio and Ruth, May 16, 1819.
Charles, s. Castalio and Ruth, Nov. 6, 1820.
Charles E., s. Leander and Sophronia, May 25, 1837.
Ebenezer Clark, s. Castalio and Ruth, July 4, 1806.
Elias Pool, s. Castalio and Ruth, Mar. 11, 1810.
Eliza, d. Leander and Sophronia, Apr. 24, 1827.
Eliza Jane, d. Joseph and Martha, Apr. 28, 1839.
Ellen Marrion, d. Benjamin G. and Olive C., Oct. 6, 1844.
Frederic, s. Castalio and Mary (b. Townsend), June —, 1848.
George, s. Gustavus and Julia, July 7, 1822.
Grenville, s. Castalio and Ruth, Sept. 25, 1822.
Henry, s. Leander and Sophronia, Nov. 18, 1818.
Inez, d. Benjamin G. and Olive, ——— [rec. June 19, 1847].
Jerome, s. Leander and Sophronia, Oct. 21, 1834.
Laura, d. Castalio and Ruth, May 19, 1817.
Lucinda, d. Castalio and Ruth, May 12, 1814.
Sarah, d. Castalio and Ruth, Dec. 21, 1811.
Thomas B., s. Leander and Sophronia, Aug. 27, 1822.
William E., s. Leander and Sophronia, Oct. 16, 1829.

HUITCHOSON (see Hutchinson, Hutchoson), John (Huitchson), s. Benjamen and Sarah, Nov. 27, 1737.

HUTCHINSON (see Huitchoson, Hutchoson), Benjamin, s. Hezekiah and Rachel, June 23, 1812.
Betsey Salvina, d. Hezekiah and Rachel, June 2, 1814.
Bettey, d. Benj[amin] and Rebekah, Jan. 20, 1760.

HUTCHINSON, Eliza Susannah, d. Hes[e]k[ia]h and Rachel, Sept. 27, 1826.
Elmira, d. Hezekiah and Rachel, Apr. 10, 1816.
Hezekiah Albin, s. Hezekiah and Rachel, Apr. 10, 1809.
John, s. Benj[amin] and Rebekah, June 29, 1757.
John Gould, s. Hez[e]k[iah] and Rachel, July 21, 1822.
Lucy, d. Hezekiah and Rachel, Sept. 20, 1820.
Molley, d. Benjamin Jr. and Rebekah, Aug. 21, 1751.
Rachel Ann, d. Hezekiah and Rachel, July 2, 1818.
Rebekah, d. Benj[amin] and Rebekah, Feb. 10, 1762.
Sarah, d. Benj[amin] [and] Rebekah, Nov. 9, 1765.
Selina Ann, d. Hezekiah and Rachel, Mar. 3, 1808.
Susanna, d. Benj[amin] and Rebekah, Aug. 8, 1754.

HUTCHOSON (see Huitchoson, Hutchinson), Bartholomew, [twin] s. Benjamen (Huitchoson) and Sarah, July 5, 1734.
Mary, [twin] d. Benjamen (Huitchoson) and Sarah, July 5, 1734.

HYDE, Mary Payson, d. Rev. George C. and Henrietta M. of Syracuse, N.Y., July 19, 1847.

JACKSON, Josiah Newton, s. Joshua (b. Oxford, " M E.") and Mary (b. Lexington), Aug. 24, 1848.

JOHNSON, Abby Maria, d. Obidiah P. and Abigail, June 21, 1845.
Ella, d. Obidiah P. and Abigail, Dec. 29, 1846.
——, d. Ira and Arabella, Jan. —, 1844.

JONES, Betsey, d. Col. Timothy and Rebekah, May 26, 1790.
Charles Henry, s. Ephriam and Eliza B., Apr. 7, 1845.
Daniel, s. Daniel and Mary, Nov. 13, 1773.
Ebenezer, s. Ebenezer and Mary, Mar. 29, 1752.
Ebenezer, s. Ebenezer and Mary, Aug. 5, 1761.
Ephraim, [twin] s. Ebenezer and Mary, Apr. 17, 1758.
Frederick, s. Timothy and Susan, Feb. 4, 1811.
Hanah, d. James Cary and Mary, Dec. 26, 1787.
Hephzibah, d. Eben[eze]r and Mary, Oct. 29, 1756.
Isaac, s. Timothy and Rebekah, May 24, 1782.
Isaac, s. Col. Timothy and Rebekah, July 21, 1796.
Joel Francis, s. Elbridge and Abigail, Oct. 1, 1837.
John, s. Timothy and Rebekah, Oct. 12, 1773.
John, s. Timothy and Susan, Aug. 1, 1815.
Lucy, [twin] d. Ebenezer and Mary, Apr. 17, 1758.
Lucy, d. Timothy and Rebekah, Nov. 30, 1777.
Mary, d. Ebenezer and Mary, Sept. 9, 1754.

JONES, Nabby, d. Timothy and Rebekah, Oct. 13, 1771.
Nathan, s. Ebenezer and Mary, Apr. 21, 1753.
Oliver, s. James Cary and Mary, Oct. 24, 1789.
Polley, d. Timothy and Rebekah, Nov. 17, 1769.
Rebecca, d. Timothy and Susan, Sept. 9, 1818.
Saley, d. Capt. Timothy and Rebekah, Aug. 9, 1786.
Samuel, s. Daniel and Mary, Mar. 5, 1772.
Samuel, s. James Cary and Mary, May 21, 1792.
Susan, d. Timothy and Susan, Feb. 8, 1809.
Susan, d. Timothy and Susan, June 28, 1813.
Sylvania, d. Col. Timothy and Rebekah, June 17, 1793.
Timothy, s. Timothy and Rebekah, Mar. 27, 1780.
Timothy, s. Timothy and Susanna, Nov. 19, 1806.

KELLEY, ———, d. Jacob and Anna, Apr. 17, 1848.

KENT, Isac, s. Isac and Anne, Oct. 23, 1730.

KIDDER, Benjamin, s. Benjamin and Hannah, June 13, 1734.
Hanah, d. Ben[j]amin and Hannah, July 8, 1735.
Hannah, d. Benjamin and Hannah, Aug. 10, 1732.
Hannah, d. Benjamin and Hannah, June 6, 1736.
Hannah, d. Benjam[in] and Hannah, Jan. 28, 1738-9.
Mary, d. Benjamin and Judith, Aug. 5, 1755, in Billerica.

KILLAM, Sarah Wyman, d. Frederick D. and Sarah C., Sept. 5, 1843.

KINSMAN, Allice Elizsa, d. Timo[thy] and Lucy, July 24, 1813, in Linn.
George Shattuck, s. Timothy and Lucy S., Aug. 5, 1809.
Lucy Angeline, d. Timo[thy] and Lucy, Sept. 8, 1811, in Reading.
Martha Maria, d. Timothy and Lucy, Apr. 20, 1815.
Moses Abbott, s. Timothy and Lucy, Mar. 5, 1817.

LANE, Abigail French, d. Solomon and Sarah, Mar. 23, 1799.
Abigail Rebeckah, d. Oliver W. and Catherine, June 3, 1826.
Abner, s. Ens. John and Ruhamah, Apr. 18, 1786.
Abner Bridge, s. Eliab B. and Anna, May 24, 1806.
Alonzo, s. Seth and Amorille, July 5, 1838.
Amasa, s. Ens. John and Ruhamah, Apr. 30, 1790.
Amittai, d. Job and Susanna, Feb. 9, 1759.
Amittai Bacon, d. David and Molly, July 26, 1793.
Andrew, s. Job and Mary, ———, 1820.
Anna, d. Timothy and Lydia, Mar. 30, 1758.

LANE, Anna, d. Solomon and Sarah, Aug. 19, 1782.
Arinda, d. Jonathan and Hannah, May 26, 1793.
Benjamin, s. John Jr. and Ruth, Mar. 17, 1754.
Bethiah, d. Job and Susanna, Feb. 1, 1764.
Caroline, d. Roger and Zelina, May 5, 1831.
Catharine W., d. Eliab B. and Anna, Sept. 2, 1809.
Catherine Amelia, d. Oliver W. and Catherine, Dec. 4, 1823.
Chandler Bridge, s. Abner and Lydia, May 3, 1837.
Charles, s. Jonathan and Hannah, Aug. 4, 1804.
Daniel, s. Samuel and Hannah, Oct. 9, 1774.
Daniel, s. Solomon and Sarah, Nov. 5, 1800.
David, s. James and Martha, Mar. 17, 1733.
David, s. James and Mary, Mar. 11, 1759.
David, s. David and Molly, Sept. 17, 1796.
David Woodard, s. Samuel 2d and Lucy, Oct. 28, 1801.
Dorcas, d. Samuel Jr. and Elizabeth, Feb. 18, 1771.
Dudley, s. Luke and Mathey (Martha), Oct. 17, 1822.
Ebenezer, s. Sam[ue]ll and Ruth, May 14, 1771.
Eli, s. Roger and Zelina, Mar. 3, 1833.
Eliab, s. John and Ruhamah, June 21, 1780.
Eliot, d. John and Ruhamah, Apr. 31, 1782.
Eliot, d. Roger and Zelina, Dec. 29, 1837.
Eliza Ann, d. Eliab B. and Anna, May 17, 1804.
Elizabeth, d. Timothy and Lydia, May 7, 1753.
Emeline, d. Seth and Amorille, Jan. 27, 1829.
Emeline, d. Roger and Zelina, Sept. 17, 1835.
Enoch, s. Solomon and Sarah, Feb. 7, 1793.
Ephraim, s. Samuel and Ruth, Mar. 22, 1767.
Esther, d. John and Ruth, Mar. 1, 1758.
Fanna, d. Job and Elizabeth, May 24, 1781.
Francis, s. John Jr. and Ruth, Sept. 18, 1748.
Francis, s. John Jr. and Ruth, Aug. 31, 1750.
Galan, s. Eliab B. and Anna, Apr. 24, 1811.
George, s. Jonathan and Hannah, May 8, 1802.
George, s. Roger and Zelina, Aug. 7, 1827.
George Winchester, s. Abner B. and Lydia, July 25, 1829.
Gersham Flagg, s. John "Ter^s" [*tertius*] and Martha, July 30, 1753.
Grace, d. John Jr. and Ruhamah, Dec. 22, 1777.
Hanna, [twin] d. Lt. Job and Martha, Sept. 22, 1733.
Hannah, d. Capt. John and Hannah, May 16, 1734.
Hannah, d. Job Jr. and Susanna, Jan. 31, 1754.
Hannah, d. John "Ter^s" [*tertius*] and Martha, May 13, 1755.
Hannah, d. Samuel and Elizabeth, Feb. 26, 1765.

LANE, Hannah, d. Samuel and Hannah, Apr. 6, 1776.
Hannah, d. Ziba and Hannah, Nov. 25, 1778.
Hannah, d. Jonathan and Hannah, Oct. 11, 1789.
Hannah, d. Luke and Hannah, May 4, 1799.
Hannah A., d. Job and Mary, Nov. 22, 1818.
Henry Francis, s. Oliver W. and Catherine, Sept. 4, 1839.
Henry Watson, s. Abner B. and Lydia, Mar. 16, 1831.
Hepzibah, d. John " Ter^s " [*tertius*] and Martha, Aug. 30, 1761.
Isaac, s. James and Mary, May 13, 1766.
James, s. James Jr. and Mary, Mar. 10, 1754.
James, s. David and Molley, July 15, 1799.
Jesse, s. Ens. John and Ruhamah, Mar. 25, 1788.
Job, ch. Lt. Job and Martha, Sept. 27, 1718, " before Bedford was nown."
Job, s. Job "Trs" [*tertius*] and Sarah, Feb. 14, 1741–2.
Job, s. Job Jr. and Susanna, June 13, 1756.
Job, s. David and Molly, Apr. 3, 1789.
Job, s. Luke and Hannah, Aug. 7, 1794.
Job Blanchard, s. David Jr. and Betsey, Oct. 18, 1828.
John, ch. Lt. Job and Martha, Oct. 2, 1720, " before Bedford was nown."
John, s. John and Ruth, Dec. 7, 1746.
John, s. Capt. John and Ruhamah, July 5, 1784.
John Roger, s. Roger and Zelina, July 10, 1824.
Jonas, s. Samuel and Ruth, May 10, 1761.
Jonathan, s. Job 3d and Sarah, Feb. 3, 1743–4.
Jonathan, s. John and Sarah, Oct. 15, 1763.
Jonathan Jr., s. Jonathan and Hannah, Jan. 27, 1788. [" fifth generation from Job Lane, the head of the family in this country," G.R.]
Jonathan Abbott, s. Jonathan and Ruhamah, Oct. 23, 1818.
Jonathan Abbott, s. Jona[than] and Ruhamah, May 15, 1822.
Joseph, s. Joseph and Thankful, Sept. 6, 1736.
Josiah, s. John Jr. and Sarah, Feb. 25, 1762.
Josiah, s. Ziba and Hannah, Sept. 28, 1780.
Josiah, s. Solomon and Sarah, July 9, 1785.
Josiah Abbot, s. Jonathan and Hannah, Aug. 17, 1791.
Josiah Stearns, s. Solomon and Sarah, Nov. 11, 1787.
Josiah Stearns, s. Josiah S. and Amelia, Dec. 29, 1813.
Laura Ann, d. Oliver W. and Catherine, July 21, 1830.
Laura Ann, d. Oliver W. and Catherine, May 1, 1834.
Lavinia, d. Roger and Zelina, July 9, 1842.
Love, d. James and Martha, Jan. 8, 1728–9.
Luce, d. Job [and] Martha, May 3, 1732.

LANE, Lucy, d. Timothy and Lydia, Nov. 7, 1751.
Lucy Rebeckah, d. Samuel 2d and Lucy, Mar. 31, 1808.
Luke, s. Job and Susanna, Sept. 29, 1768.
Luke, s. Luke and Hannah, Sept. 9, 1791.
Lydia, d. Job Jr. and Susanna, Aug. 13, 1749.
Lydia, d. Timothy and Lydia, Dec. 16, 1760.
Lydia, d. Tim[oth]y and Lydia, Jan. 16, 1772.
Lydia Harriet, d. Stephen and Allice, Mar. 26, 1808.
Marcy, d. James and Martha, Dec. 24, 1730.
Martha, ch. Lt. Job and Martha, June 22, 1716, "before Bedford was nown."
Martha, d. John "Ter^s" [*tertius*] and Martha, Aug. 13, 1748.
Mary, ch. Lt. Job and Martha, Feb. 24, 1725, "before Bedford was nown."
Mary, d. Job Jr. and Sarah, Mar. 16, 1747–8.
Mary Ann, d. Samuel 2d and Lucy, Nov. 24, 1803.
Mary Ann, d. David Jr. and Betsey, Aug. 2, 1826.
Mary Eleanor, d. William A. and Mary (b. Pepperell), Feb. 25, 1849.
Mary Elizabeth, d. Job and Mary, Mar. 5, 1816.
Mary Maria, d. Roger and Zelina, July 7, 1826.
Mary Priscilia, d. Eliab B. and Anna, Oct. 12, 1812.
Mary Whiting, d. Oliver W. and Catherine, Mar. 31, 1820.
Matthew, s. John and Martha, Oct. 8, 1750.
Molley, d. Job and Susanna, June 14, 1761.
Molly, d. David and Molly, Apr. 23, 1782.
Nathan, s. Timothy and Lydia, Feb. 11, 1768.
Olive, d. Job and Mary, Apr. 9, 1817.
Oliver Josiah, s. Oliver W. and Catherine, Jan. 29, 1828.
Oliver Wellington, s. James Jr. and Mary, Oct. 27, 1751.
Oliver Wellington, s. Solomon and Sarah, June 16, 1794.
Pata, d. Samuel and Hannah, Aug. 19, 1780.
Patta, d. Timothy and Lydia, Nov. 8, 1765.
Phebe, d. Samuel Jr. and Elizabeth, Feb. 12, 1773.
Polley, d. Samuel Jr. and Elizabeth, Aug. 15, 1776.
Rebekah, d. Samu[e]ll and Ruth, Jan. 17, 1763.
Reuben Bacon, s. Seth and Amerille, Jan. 18, 1831, in Lexington.
Rhoda, d. Timothy and Lydia, May 17, 1763.
Rollin, s. Jonathan and Hannah, Apr. 9, 1795.
Ruhamah, d. John and Ruhamah, June 10, 1775.
Ruhamah, d. Jonathan and Ruhamah, May 6, 1816.
Ruth, d. John Jr. and Ruth, Apr. 8, 1752.
Ruth, d. Sam[ue]ll and Ruth, June 7, 1769.
Sally, d. Sollomon and Sarah, Apr. 30, 1789.

BEDFORD BIRTHS. 37

LANE, Samuel, s. James and Martha, July 11, 1737.
Samuel, s. John and Hannah, Oct. 21, 1737.
Samuel, s. Job and Sarah, May 6, 1746.
Samuel, s. Samuel and Hannah, Jan. 15, 1778.
Samuel John, s. Jonathan and Hannah, Jan. 15, 1808.
Samuel Leavitt, s. Oliver W. and Catherine, Feb. 24, 1838.
Samuel Richardson, s. Samuel 2d and Lucy, Feb. 26, 1806.
Samuel Wright, s. Jona[than] and Ruhamah, Aug. 2, 1820.
Sarah, [twin] d. Lt. Job and Martha, Sept. 22, 1733.
Sarah, d. Job " Trs " [*tertius*] and Sarah, Jan. 28, 1739-40.
Sarah, d. Job Jr. and Susanna, Dec. 15, 1751.
Sarah, d. John and Sarah, Oct. 1, 1765.
Sarah, d. Jonathan and Hannah, May 1, 1797.
Sarah Elizabeth, d. Oliver W. and Catherine, Nov. 27, 1818.
Seth, s. Luke and Hannah, Aug. 9, 1796.
Silvana, d. David and Molly, Sept. 17, 1801.
Solomon, s. James Jr. and Mary, Aug. 7, 1756.
Sophronia, d. Roger and Zelina, Sept. 21, 1840.
Stephen, s. Timothy and Lydia, Aug. 20, 1755.
Susan, d. Roger and Zelina, Nov. 20, 1836.
Susan Grace, d. Eliab B. and Anna, Jan. 22, 1808.
Susana, d. Job 3d and Susana, Dec. 21, 1747.
Susanna, d. James and Martha, Jan. 18, 1735-6.
Susanna, d. David and Molly, Oct. 14, 1785.
Timothy, ch. Lt. Job and Martha, July 10, 1722, " before Bedford was nown."
Whippel, ch. Lt. Job and Martha, Sept. 5, 1727, " before Bedford was nown."
William, s. Job and Mary, ———— [rec. after ch. b. ———, 1820].
William Augustus, s. Oliver W. and Catherine, Mar. 12, 1822.
Ziba, s. John and Ruth, July 5, 1756.
Ziba, s. Ziba and Hannah, Jan. 31, 1782.

LAWRENCE, Charles Frederick, s. Sylvanus and Malvina, Apr. 7, 1840.
George Otis, s. Sylvanus and Malvina, Jan. 22, 1843.

LITCHFIELD, Joseph Warren, s. Joseph and Theresa, Sept. 11, 1847.
Marion Eliza, d. Joseph and Theresa, July 5, 1846.

MANNING, Elizabeth Iogene, d. Charles E. (b. Merrimack, N.H.) and Malvina, Mar. 11, 1849.

MANSFEELD (see Mansfeld, Mansfeld), Mary, d. John and Rachel, Nov. 8, 1727.

MANSFELD (see Mansfeeld, Mansfield), Abigail, d. John and Rachel, Nov. 8, 1729.
John, s. John and Rachel, Mar. 5, 1734-5.

MANSFIELD (see Mansfeeld, Mansfeld), Elbridge Bacon, s. Joil and Maria L., Nov. 16, 1847.
Mary Louisa, d. Joel (b. Chelmsford) and Maria, Sept. 10, 1849.

MARSHALL, Abel, s. William and Elizabeth, Apr. 9, 1740.
Sarah, d. William and Elizabeth, Apr. 21, 1743.

MAXWELL, Dorcas, d. Hugh and Bridget, Apr. 13, 1765.
Edwin, s. Francis B. and Susanna, Feb. 10, 1814.
Frances [sic] Bowman, s. William and Sarah, Feb. 1, 1786.
Francis, s. Francis B. and Susanna, Nov. 5, 1812.
Hannah, d. Hugh and Bridget, June 22, 1761.
Hugh, s. Hugh and Bridget, Mar. 13, 1770.
Lilie, d. Hugh and Bridget, Aug. 7, 1763.
Molley, d. William and Sarah, Nov. 12, 1777.
Priscilla, d. Hugh and Bridget, Oct. 23, 1767.
Rebeckah Willson, d. William and Sarah, Jan. 4, 1783, in Dublin.
Rhoda, Apr. 25, 1794. G.R.
Sarah, d. William and Sarah, Dec. 19, 1789.
William, s. William and Sarah, Mar. 30, 1776.

McCLUSKEY, ———, s. John and w., July 26, 1847.

MEAD (see Meed, Meeds), Artemas, s. Asa and Nabby, Dec. 23, 1817.
Asa, s. Asa and Naby, Feb. 4, 1804.
John Eames, s. Asa and Nabby, June 16, 1811.
Lois, d. Asa and Nabby, Jan. 14, 1815.
Lydia Abigail, d. Asa and Nabby, Mar. 7, 1806.
Stephen, s. Asa and Nabby, June 25, 1808.
Timothy Walker, s. Asa and Nabby, May 11, 1813.

MEED (see Mead, Meeds), Eunice, d. Jos[e]ph an[d] Elizabe[th], Sept. 24, 1745.

MEEDS (see Mead, Meed), Anna, d. Stephen and Desire, June 12, 1769.
Asa, s. Stephen and Desire, May 14, 1774.
Bettee, d. Joseph (Meed) and Elizabeth, June 4, 1756.
Edward, s. Joseph Jr. and Lucy, July 4, 1773.
Eli, s. Joseph and Elizabeth, Mar. 17, 1754.
Elizabeth, d. Stephen and Desire, Oct. 29, 1767.

MEEDS, Ephraim, s. Joseph Jr. and Lucy, Mar. 26, 1771.
Esther, d. Stephen and Desire, Jan. 31, 1776.
John, s. Stephen and Desire, Aug. 15, 1777.
Joseph, s. Joseph and Elizabeth, Feb. 25, 1740-1.
Joseph, s. Joseph Jr. and Lucy, Oct. 20, 1767.
Lucy, d. Joseph Jr. and Lucy, July 15, 1769.
Lydia, d. Stephen and Desire, July 15, 1771.
Patte, d. Joseph Jr. and Lucy, Feb. 21, 1777.
Ruth, d. Joseph and Elizabeth, Mar. 19, 1752.
Samuel, s. Joseph and Elizabeth, May 18, 1749.
Simeon, s. Joseph Jr. and Lucy, May 8, 1775.
Stephen, s. Joseph and Elezabth, Jan. 26, 1736-7.
Stephen, s. Stephen and Desire, Dec. 9, 1765.

MERIAM (see Merriam), Abigail, d. John and Abigail, Apr. 28, 1746.
Abraham, s. Abraham and Hannah, Feb. 14, 1779.
Anna, d. John and Abigal, July 13, 1737.
Anna Page, d. William and Rebekah, May 2, 1790.
Eleazer, s. Isaac and Sarah, Sept. 12, 1740.
Hannah, d. John and Hannah, Apr. 4, 1764.
Hannah, d. Samuel and Allice, July 23, 1799.
Isac, s. Isac and Sarah, Aug. 30, 1737.
John, s. John and Rebecca, Feb. 13, 1734-5.
John, s. John and Hannah, Aug. 28, 1774.
Jonas, s. Abraham and Hannah, Nov. 20, 1777.
Jonas, s. Samuel and Allise, Aug. 22, 1787.
Josephus, s. William and Esther, Mar. 11, 1781.
Josephus, s. William and Esther (Merriam), Mar. 10, 1785.
Louisa How, d. William and Rebekah, Oct. 2, 1792.
Lucy, d. Samuel and Allis, ——— [rec. after ch. b. June 23, 1795].
Lydia, d. John and Abigail, Apr. 6, 1742.
Lydia, d. Abraham and Hannah, Nov. 8, 1781.
Mary, d. John and Abigal, July 25, 1733.
Mary, d. Samuel and Allis, Apr. 4, 1791.
Nathaniel, s. Samuel and Allis, June 23, 1795.
Nathanil, s. John and Abigal, Dec. 15, 1739.
Rebecah, d. John and Abigal, Sept. 28, 1731.
Rebecca, d. William and Rebekah, Nov. 23, 1786, in Lexington.
Rebekah, d. John and Hannah, July 23, 1762.
Rebekah, d. John and Hannah, Mar. 25, 1766.
Salle, d. Samuel and Allis, Apr. 17, 1785.

MERIAM, Sarah, d. Isaac and Sarah, Feb. 6, 1738-9.
Thaddeus, s. John and Abigail, Apr. 17, 1748.
Thomas, s. Samuel and Allis, Jan. 26, 1793.
William, s. John Esq. and Abigail, Aug. 25, 1750.
William Bellamy, s. William and Esther, Aug. 5, 1776.
William Bellamy, s. William and Esther, Feb. 2, 1779.

MERRIAM (see Meriam), Adaline, d. Jonas and Nancy, July 24, 1812.
Eldridge, s. John and Mary, Feb. 8, 1802.
Esther, d. William and Esther, Nov. 1, 1771.
Hiram Reed, s. John and Mary, Aug. 5, 1808.
Isaac, s. Jonas and Nancy, June 23, 1809.
John, s. John A. and Nancy, May 15, 1843.
John Augustus, s. John and Mary, Dec. 20, 1803.
John Eldridge, s. Eldridge and Eliot, Oct. 13, 1824.
Lucretia Eliot, d. Eldridge and Eliot, Nov. 9, 1827.
Mary Addeline, d. John and Mary, Mar. 3, 1806.
Mary Adeline, d. John and Mary, Jan. 28, 1812.
Mary Adeline, d. Eldridge and w., Apr. 9, 1844.
Nancy, d. John A. and Nancy, ——— [rec. June 19, 1847].
Olive, d. Nathaniel and Olive, Mar. 1, 1763.
Samuel, s. Nathaniel (Meriam) and Olive, Nov. 5, 1749.
Sarah, d. Nathaniel and Olive, Oct. 10, 1753.
Susan Frances, d. John and Mary, Oct. 20, 1818.

MERRITT, Helen, d. Edward and Betsey O., Mar. 28, 1845.

MONROE (see Munroe), Caroline French, twin ch. Jonas and Mary Ann, Apr. 21, 1839.
Catherine Frances, twin ch. Jonas and Mary Ann, Apr. 21, 1839.
Ellen Maria, d. Jonas and Abigail F., Aug. 30, 1832.
George Henry, s. Jonas and Mary Ann, Nov. 15, 1835.
George Wright, s. Abel S. and Sarah, Sept. 26, 1838.
Jonas Edward, s. Jonas and Mary Ann, May 4, 1837.
Sarah Eliza, d. Abel and Caroline, Jan. 13, 1846.
Sophronia Adelini, d. Abel L. and Sarah, Dec. 26, 1841.

MOOR (see Moore), John, s. John and Elesabth, Mar. 16, 1729.
Joseph, s. John (Morr) and Elezabath, Mar. 24, 1732.

MOORE (see Moor), Elizabeth, d. Joseph and Dorcas, Oct. 30, 1753.
Elizabeth, d. John and Mary, Aug. 12, 1759.
Lydia, d. John and Mary, May 17, 1765.
Mary, d. John and Mary, Nov. 2, 1761.

MUNROE (see Monroe), ———, d. Josiah and Susanna of Lexington, Dec. 25, 1768.

NEWTON, Ellis, d. Simon and Amittai, June 6, 1755.

PAGE (see Paige), Almira, d. John and Esther, Dec. 26, 1797.
Anna, d. Ebenezer and Dorothy, Sept. 29, 1760, in Lexington.
Anna Pricellah, d. John and Esther, Apr. 9, 1808.
Araza, s. John and Esther, Aug. 9, 1800.
Asseneth Goult, d. Joshua and Nancy, Aug. 20, 1824.
Bellamy, s. John and Esther, Dec. 5, 1802.
Benjamin, [twin] s. Nathaniel and Sarah, Mar. 3, 1781.
Benjamin, s. Nathaniel Jr. and Lydia, Jan. 15, 1814.
Benjamin Franklin, s. Benjamin and Mary, May 28, 1844.
Caroline Matilda, ch. Larkin P. and Rebecca, Sept. 20, 1833.
Charles Parker, s. Larkin P. and Rebecca, Aug. 31, 1830.
Christopher, [twin] s. Nathaniel and Sarah, Dec. 10, 1783.
Clariat, d. John and Esther, May 4, 1794.
Cyrus, s. Nath[anie]l Jr. and Lydia, Nov. 28, 1801.
Cyrus Andrew, s. Cyrus and Susan E., June 9, 1845.
Daniel Harrington, s. Timothy and Isanna, Jan. 4, 1819.
David, s. "cor^t." Nath[anie]ll Jr. and Hannah, Apr. 4, 1740.
David, s. David and Abigail, Feb. 7, 1767.
David, s. Nathaniel Jr. and Lydia, Sept. 4, 1811.
Dolley, d. Ebenezer and Dorithy, Dec. 11, 1768.
Dorcas, d. Timothy and Margaret, Apr. 22, 1775.
Ebenezer, s. Ebenezer and Dorothy, Mar. 30, 1765, in Lexington.
Eliza C., Aug. 20, 1846 [?].
Elizabeth, d. Christopher and Elizabeth, Oct. 3, 1731.
Esther Bellamy, d. John and Esther, Feb. 12, 1796.
Eveline Rebecca, ch. Larkin P. and Rebecca, Jan. 19, 1832.
Fidaliea, d. Nathaniel Jr. and Lydia, July 9, 1803.
Grovener Abijah, ch. Larkin P. and Rebecca, Aug. 6, 1842.
Hannah, d. David and Abigail, Mar. 11, 1773.
Harriet Fidelia [dup. F.], d. Cyrus and Susan [dup. adds E.], Nov. 13, 1847.
Harriet Jane, d. Joshua and Nancy, June 28, 1823.
Henrietta, d. Cyrus and Susan E., May 21, 1843.
Henry Larkin [ch. Larkin P. and Rebecca], Jan. 10, 1836.
Isaac Fitch, s. Nathaniel Jr. and Lydia, Aug. 30, 1805.
Isanna, d. Thomas Jr. and Betsey, Apr. 12, 1809.
Isanna Harrington [ch. Larkin P. and Rebecca], Nov. 16, 1843.
John, s. Ebenezer and Dorothy, Feb. 18, 1767, in Lexington.
John, [twin] s. Nathaniel and Sarah, Mar. 3, 1781.
John Flint, ch. Larkin P. and Rebecca, Aug. 24, 1838.

PAGE, John Henry, s. Silas W. and Betsey B., Aug. 18, 1839.
Joseph Augustus, s. David and Eliza, ——— [rec. Aug. 24, 1846].
Joseph W., s. Timothy and Margaret, May 16, 1767.
Joshua, s. Ebenezer and Dorithy, Jan. 18, 1779.
Larkin Pierce, s. Timothy and Isanna, Sept. 24, 1802.
Louisa Howe, d. John and Esther, July 17, 1806.
Lucretia, d. Joshua and Betsey, Aug. 25, 1829.
Lucy, d. Ebenezer and Dorothy, July 11, 1772.
Mary Ann, d. Joshua and Elsey, Aug. 12, 1816.
Molley, d. Ebenezer and Dorothy, July 24, 1774.
Moses, s. Ebenezer and Dorothy, Sept. 11, 1770.
Moses, s. Ebenezer and Susanna, Oct. 9, 1784.
Moses, s. William and Lucy, May 16, 1816.
Nancy Waterman, d. Joshua and Nancy, Apr. 16, 1826.
Nathaniel, s. Nathaniel Jr. and Sarah, Oct. 25, 1775.
Nathaniel, s. Nathaniel Jr. and Lydia, May 16, 1807.
Nathaniel, s. Nathaniel Jr. and Lydia, May 3, 1809.
Rebekah, d. Ebenezer and Dorothy, June 9, 1763, in Lexington.
Ruhamah, [twin] d. Nathaniel and Sarah, May 1, 1788. [w. Jonathan Lane, G.R.]
Sally Maria, d. Joshua and Sally, Nov. 20, 1814.
Samuel, s. Nath[anie]l and Lydia, May —, 1816.
Sarah, d. Nathaniel Jr. and Sarah, May 22, 1777.
Sarah Augusta, ch. Larkin P. and Rebecca, Apr. 4, 1841.
Sarah Eveline, d. Joshua and Sally, Aug. 8, 1808.
Susanna, d. Moses and Hannah, Apr. 12, 1828.
Susanna Simonds, d. William and Lucy, June 2, 1818.
Susanna Simonds, d. William and Lucy, Oct. 24, 1823.
Thaddeus, [twin] s. Nathaniel and Sarah, May 1, 1788.
Thomas, [twin] s. Nathaniel and Sarah, Dec. 10, 1783.
Timothy, s. "cor^t." John and Rebackah, June 11, 1741.
Timothy, s. Lt. Timothy and Isanna, Dec. 18, 1810.
Warren, s. Cyrus and Susan E., June 9, 1845.
William, s. Ebenezer and Susana, Mar. 19, 1783.
William Edward, s. Larkin P. and Rebecca, Feb. 23, 1847.
———, d. Larkin P. and w., Nov. 16, 1843

PAIGE (see Page), Abigal, d. Natha[nie]ll Jr. and Hannah, Sept. 5, 1745.
Christ[o]p[he]r, s. Christ[o]p[he]r and Susanna, Oct. 29, 1743.
Ebenezar, s. John and Rebecca, June 3, 1737.
Elizabeth, d. John and Rebakah, Aug. 3, 1748.
Hannah (Paig), d. Nathaneil and Hannah, May 15, 1736.
James, s. John and Rebecca, May 12, 1735.

PAIGE, Joana, d. John and Rebakah, June 15, 1746.
Job, s. Christopher and Susana, May 31, 1748.
John, s. John and Rebecca, Sept. 2, 1733.
Luce, d. Christopher and Elizabeth, Feb. 22, 1733-4.
Lucy, d. Christopher and Susanna, Mar. 26, 1752.
Mary, d. John and Rebakah, July 1, 1745.
Mary, d. Christopher and Susanna, Feb. 20, 1746-7.
Mary, d. John and Rebekah, Oct. 9, 1753.
Nathanil, s. "Cor^t." John and Rebakah, June 20, 1742.
Rebakah, d. John and Rebakah, Aug. 23, 1743.
Samuel, s. "Co^r." John and Rebekah, Aug. 1, 1751.
Sarah, d. John and Rebakah, June 8, 1747.
Susanna, d. "Cor^t." John (Page) and Rebakah, Oct. 21, 1739.
Susanna, d. "Cor^t." Nath[an]il Jr. and Hannah, Jan. 22, 1742.
Susanna, d. Christopher and Susanna, May 17, 1745.
Susanna, d. Christopher and Susanna, Apr. 7, 1750.
Susanna, d. "Co^r." John and Rebekah, June 12, 1750.
Thomas, s. Nathanel and Hanna, May 5, 1733.
William, s. Nathanel and Hannah, Feb. 19, 1737-8.

PARKER, Clarissa Maria, d. Daniel (b. Billerica) and Mary, June 2, 1848.

PARKHURST, Joseph Addison, s. Joseph and Rhoda, Jan. 31, 1808.
Sylvester, s. Joseph and Rhoda, June 24, 1810.

PEARCE (see Pierce).

PENNAMAN (see Penniman), Prisa, d. Rev. Joseph and Hannah, Apr. 22, 1787.

PENNIMAN (see Pennaman), Hannah, d. Rev. Joseth and Hannah, Aug. 11, 1772.
Lucy, d. Rev. J. [and Hannah], Aug. 7, 1778.
Molly, d. Rev. Joseph and Hannah, Feb. 18, 1775.
Polly, d. Rev. J. [and Hannah], Oct. 17, 1781.

PERRY (see Pery), Asa, s. Thomas and Abigail, Dec. 12, 1754.
Elizebeth, d. Thomas and Abigail, Sept. 10, 1766.
Micah, s. Thomas and Abigail, Dec. 3, 1759.
Thaddeus, s. Thomas and Abigail, Apr. 13, 1761.

PERY (see Perry), Oliver, s. Thomas and Abigail, June 11, 1769.

PHELPS, Emma Elvira, d. Joseph and Drusilla, Oct. 27, 1846.

PHELPS, Joseph Thomas, s. Joseph (b. Wilton, N. H.) and Dusilla (b. Hudson, N.H.), Nov. 14, 1848.
Lorenzo Fremont, s. Lorenzo and Susanna, Dec. 19, 1847.

PIERCE, Joseph, s. Augustus and Ruth, Oct. 22, 1843.

PIPER, Abigail Lawrence, d. William and Elizabeth, Jan. 30, 1831.
Charles Alonzo, d. [sic] Daniel B. and Elizabeth, Mar. 27, 1847.
Daniel, s. Daniel (b. Waltham) and Elizabeth H. (b. N. Y.), June 1, 1848.
Daniel Alonzo, s. Daniel (b. Waltham) and Elizabeth H. (b. N. Y.), Aug. 25, 1849.
Zylpha, d. Daniel B. and Elizabith, Jan. 15, 1845.

POLARD (see Pollard), Dorety, d. Walter and Dorety, June 23, 1737.
Oliver (Polord), s. Oliver and Hannah, Jan. 27, 1736–7.

POLLARD (see Polard), Benjamin, s. Walter and Dorrithy, July 18, 1745.
Bettee, d. Walter and Dorithy, Nov. 12, 1750.
Caroline Rebecca, d. Oliver and Rachel L., Aug. 20, 1837.
David, s. Walter and Dorrithy, Nov. 22, 1739.
Hannah, d. Oliver and Hannah, Nov. 23, 1739.
Hannah Elizabeth, d. Obed and Hannah, Jan. 1, 1818.
Jacob Osgood, s. Obed and Hannah, Jan. 10, 1816.
James, s. Walter and Dorrithy, Sept. 14, 1743.
James, s. James and Molley, Dec. 23, 1766, in Chelmsford.
James, s. Obed and Hannah, Jan. 24, 1820.
Jane, d. Oliver and Mary, Nov. 24, 1780.
Jonathan, s. Walter and Dorrithy, Sept. 21, 1741.
Jonathan, s. Jonathan and Mary, May 10, 1771.
Jonathan, s. Obed and Hannah, Oct. 31, 1810.
Josiah, s. Obed and Hannah, June 27, 1813.
Lucy, d. Ollever and Hannah, Jan. 17, 1742.
Lucy, d. Walter and Dorithy, Mar. 2, 1748–9.
Lydia, d. Jonathan and Mary, June 21, 1768.
Mary, d. Oliver and Mary, Dec. 29, 1787.
Matthew, s. Oliver and Hannah, Dec. 23, 1749.
Molle, d. Jonathan and Mary, July 3, 1765.
Molley, d. Oliver and Hannah, June 5, 1752.
Obed, s. [Oliver] and Mary, Oct. 18, 1783.
Olive, d. Walter and Dorithy, July 12, 1753.
Oliver, s. Oliver Jr. and Mary, Nov. 7, 1778.
Pattee, d. David and Pattee, Jan. 23, 1769.

BEDFORD BIRTHS. 45

POLLARD, Rachel Antenette, d. Oliver and Rachel L., Mar. 3, 1835.
Rebekah, d. Oliver and Hannah, May 5, 1746.
Samuel, s. David and Pattee, May 18, 1767.
Sarah, d. Jonathan and Mary, Aug. 26, 1766.
Sary, d. Walter and Dorrethy, June 18, 1747.
Susanna, d. David and Pattee, Mar. 18, 1772.
Thaddeus, s. Walter and Dorathy, Apr. 27, 1755.
Walter, s. Walter and Dorathy, Aug. 21, 1757.
———, s. Jonathan and Sarah, Dec. 11, 1762.

PORTER, Bethiah, d. Joseph and Bethiah, Nov. 18, 1744.
Desire, d. Joseph and Bethiah, Feb. 11, 1752.
Edith, d. Joseph and Bethiah, Mar. 1, 1754.
Israel, s. Joseph and Bethiah, Sept. 2, 1746.
Jemima, d. Joseph and Bethiah, July 8, 1750.
Joseph, s. Joseph and Bethiah, Sept. 6, 1748.
Joseph Mulliken, s. Asa and Mary, Nov. 24, 1819.
Lydia, d. Joseph and Bethiah, Sept. 15, 1761.
Mary Rebecca, d. Asa and Mary, Aug. 25, 1821.
Molly, d. Joseph and Bethiah, Apr. 23, 1743.
Oliver, d. Joseph and Bethiah, Dec. 2, 1765.
Sarah, d. Joseph and Bethiah, Sept. 29, 1756.
William, s. Joseph and Bethiah, July 7, 1759.

PRESTON, Amariah, s. Dr. Amariah and Ruhamah, June 21, 1798.
Elbridge Warren, s. Ezekiel Warren and Lucy Minerva, Nov. 8, 1824.
Ezekiel Warren, s. Dr. Amariah and Ruhamah, July 8, 1800.
Ezekiel Warren, s. Dr. Amariah and Ruhamah, Dec. 24, 1802.
George Warren, s. Ezekiel W. and Lucy Minerva, Feb. 28, 1828, "permitted to take the name of Sherman Stearns Preston by an act of the Legislature at there January Session 1841 and will hereafter be known by the name of Sherman Stearns Preston Born Janury [sic] 28 1828."
Hannah, d. Dr. Amariah and Hannah, Jan. 8, 1795.
Harvey Newton, s. Dr. Amariah and Ruhamah, June 21, 1806.
Lovice Matilda, d. Dr. Amariah and Ruhamah, Feb. 19, 1809.
Lucy Maria, d. Ezekiel and Lucy M., Dec. 11, 1826.
Marshall, s. Dr. Amariah and Hannah, June 5, 1792.
Sherman Stearns (see George Warren Preston).

PRIST, Aaron, s. Aaron (Prisst) and Martha, Sept. 14, 1781.

PROCTOR, ———, s. William and Susan, Feb. 14, 1845.

PULSIFER, Elizabeth, d. Robert and Elizabeth, Mar. 4, 1819.

PUTNAM, Benjamin, s. Israel and Sarah, Aug. 2, 1725.
Benjamin, s. Benj[ami]n and Eunice, Aug. 21, 1762.
Bredget, d. Israel and Sarah, Feb. 11, 1737.
Daniel, s. Israel Jr. and Sarah, Oct. 4, 1759.
Elijah, s. Elijah and Lucey, Feb. 16, 1804.
Elizabeth, d. Israel Jr. and Sarah, July 28, 1753.
Elizabth, d. Israel and Sarah, July 18, 1731.
Israel, s. Israel a[nd] Sarah, Mar. 20, 1723 [1722-3, written above].
Israel, s. Israel Jr. and Sarah, Apr. 27, 1755.
Israel, s. Israel Jr. and Elizabeth, Aug. 12, 1785.
John, s. Israel Jr. and Sarah, Apr. 23, 1750.
Jonas, s. Jonas and Hannah, Oct. 23, 1811.
Jonathan, s. Israel and Sarah, July 16, 1727.
Lucy Adaline, d. Elijah and Lucy, Oct. 21, 1807.
Lucy Desire, d. Jonas and Hannah, Nov. 11, 1817.
Mary, d. Dea. Israel and Sarah, Nov. 18, 1735.
Mary, d. Jona[tha]n and Hannah, Nov. 18, 1750.
Samuel Hartwell, s. Jonas and Hannah, Mar. 23, 1813.
Sarah, d. Israel [dup. Israil] and Sarah, June 29, 1729.
Zarant, s. Dea. Israel and Sarah, Sept. 2, 1733.

QUIMBY, William Robinson, s. Dyer and Rebecca, July 4, 1820.

RAMENT (see Ramond, Ramont, Raymond, Remond), Marcy, d. William and Marcy, Oct. 2, 1747.

RAMOND (see Rament, Ramont, Raymond, Remond), Hannah, d. William and Marcy, Aug. 19, 1751.
Lucy, d. Lt. Paul (Raymond) and Tabitha, Aug. 5, 1737.

RAMONT (see Rament, Ramond, Raymond, Remond), Mary, d. William and Marcy, May 10, 1746.

RANDALL, Hiram Page, s. Samuel and Sarah, Sept. 30, 1807, in Boston.
Samuel Wright, s. Samuel and Sarah, June 22, 1811.
Sarah Reed, d. Samuel and Sarah, June 29, 1809.

RAYMOND (see Rament, Ramond, Ramont, Remond), Nathan, s. Lt. Paul and Tabitha, Feb. 29, 1739-40.

REA, Elizabeth, d. Jeremiah and Bridget, Aug. 15, 1765.
Jeremiah, s. Jeremiah and Bridget, May 7, 1763.
Sarah, d. Jeremiah and Bridget, Dec. 30, 1767.

REED, Abigail, d. David Jr. and Abigail, Feb. 6, 1813.
Addeline, d. Samuel and Harriet, Jan. 8, 1835.
Ann Winship, d. Otis and Emily, Mar. 2, 1820.
Anna, d. John and Hannah, July 2, 1787.
Benjamin, s. Capt. David and Abigail, Feb. 12, 1793.
Betsey, d. Reuben and Mary, Aug. 29, 1804.
Betsey, d. Reuben and Mary, Jan. 6, 1811.
Daniel Webster, s. Samuel and Harriet, Aug. 5, 1838.
David, s. Lt. David and Hannah, May 19, 1787.
David, s. Benjamin and Sally P., June 28, 1819.
Eliot, d. John and Ruhamah, Oct. 22, 1764.
Eliot, d. Roger and Sarah, Nov. 9, 1800.
Ellen Frances, d. Ephriam and Agusta T., May 20, 1844.
George W., s. Nehimiah L. and Ann, May 28, 1825.
Grace, d. John and Ruhamah, Apr. 26, 1760.
Hannah, d. John and Ruhamah, July 8, 1769.
Hannah, d. David and Hannah, May 14, 1784.
Hannah, d. John and Hannah, Sept. 6, 1795.
Hannah Raymond, d. David Jr. [and] Abigail, Jan. 14, 1823.
Harriet Ann, d. Samuel and Harriet, Dec. 3, 1826.
Harriet Jane, d. Sam[ue]l and Harriet, Aug. 23, 1830.
Harriet S., d. Capt. John and Sally, June 30, 1808.
Hiram, s. Reuben and Mary, Jan. 31, 1808.
H. Malvina Swain, d. Otis and Emily, Sept. 21, 1824, in Lynesborough, N.H.
Isaac, s. Reuben and Mary, Feb. 24, 1798.
Jacob H., s. Nehimiah and Ann, Feb. 22, 1838.
Jessee, s. Reuben and Mary, Jan. 31, 1800.
John, s. John and Ruhamah, June 9, 1758.
John, s. David and Hannah, Mar. 23, 1772.
John, s. John Jr. and Hannah, Apr. 10, 1798.
Jonas H., s. Sam[ue]l and Harriet, Apr. 19, 1829.
Lot, s. Reuben and Mary, Jan. 19, 1792.
Louisa, d. Reuben and Mary, Feb. 22, 1802.
Lucy Pollard, d. Benjamin and Sally, Nov. 21, 1825.
Martha Fitch, d. Nathan O. and Martha S., Mar. 2, 1841.
Mary, d. Oliver and Sarah, Sept. 12, 1763.
Mary, d. Reuben and Mary, Sept. 9, 1793.
Mary, d. Asa and Esther, Mar. 8, 1818.
Mary Caroline, d. Samuel and Harriet, Mar. 21, 1828.
Mary Caroline, d. Nathan O. and Nancy, Apr. 6, 1845.
Mary Elizabeth, twin d. Oliver and Mary, Feb. 6, 1812.
Mary Jane, d. Samuel and Harriet, July 2, 1836.
Naby, d. Capt. David and Abigail, Nov. 6, 1794.

REED, Nancy E., d. Samuel and Harriet, Mar. 30, 1833.
Nathan Henry, s. Nathan O. and Nancy (b. Sharron, N.H.), May 25, 1848.
Nathan Oliver, twin s. Oliver and Mary, Feb. 6, 1812.
Oliver, s. Oliver and Sarah, Dec. 11, 1755.
Otis, s. John and Hannah, Mar. 27, 1791.
Polley, d. David and Hannah, May 31, 1777.
Poulter, s. John and Ruhamah, Feb. 18, 1767.
Reuben, s. Oliver and Sarah, Dec. 21, 1759.
Roger, s. John and Ruhamah, June 14, 1762.
Ruhamah, d. John and Ruhamah, Dec. 11, 1753.
Salley, d. Roger and Sarah, Oct. 8, 1797.
Sally, d. Reuben and Mary, Dec. 3, 1795.
Sarah, d. Oliver and Sarah, Oct. 4, 1757.
Susanna, d. Capt. David and Martha, Jan. 3, 1806.
William Danforth, s. Benjamin and Sally P., Dec. 16, 1817.
———, d. David and Hannah, Mar. 22, 1790.

REMOND (see Rament, Ramond, Ramont, Raymond), Tabenbatha, d. Paul and Tabatha, Sept. 19, 1733.

RICE, Dorcas, d. David and w., Jan. 13, 1813.
Harriet, d. David and Nancy, Jan. 14, 1823.
Sarah, d. David and w., June 22, 1811.
———, d. Moses W. and w., Mar. 6, 1849.

ROBARTSON (see Roberson), John, s. John and Mary, May 8, 1743.
Margerit, d. John and Mary, Oct. 12, 1739.
Mary, d. John and Mary, July 16, 1745.

ROBBINSON (see Robinson), Eliza, d. Jessee and Rebecca, Dec. 27, 1809.

ROBERSON (see Robartson), Ishmael, s. David and Susanna, Apr. 5, 1777.

ROBINSON (see Robbinson), Anna, d. Jesse and Rebecca, Aug. 6, 1804.
Charles, s. Jessee and Rebecca, Apr. 10, 1816.
Charles Frederick [dup. Frederic], s. Charles and Sophia B. [dup. omits B.], Sept. 15, 1844.
Ellen Sophiah, d. Charles and Sophiah B., June 11, 1842.
Martha, d. Jessee and Rebecca, Feb. 14, 1819.
Mary, d. Jessee and Rebecca, Feb. 6, 1813.
Salley (Robertson), d. Jessee and Rebecca, Aug. 26, 1800.
Walter Billings, s. Charles and Sophia, Sept. 20, 1846.

RUSSELL, Benjamin, s. Jabez and Hannah, July 15, 1764.
Caroline [ch. Royall and Roxy B.], Apr. 8, 1841, in Burlington.
Charles [ch. Royall and Roxy B.], Apr. 2, 1839, in Lexington.
George H. [ch. Royall and Roxy B.], Jan. 16, 1832, in Billerica.
Hannah, d. Jabez and Hannah, Sept. 23, 1759.
Harriet J. [ch. Royall and Roxy B.], Oct. 21, 1834.
Hiram F. [ch. Royall and Roxy B.], Dec. 22, 1836, in Lexington.
James S., s. Royall and Roxy B., Aug. 22, 1828.
John, s. Jabez and Hannah, Apr. 3, 1776.
John P., s. Royal and Clariot Page, May 26, 1823, in Billerica.
Lucy, d. Jabez and Hannah, May 11, 1767.
Lydia, d. Jabez and Hannah, Apr. 1, 1773.
Molley, d. Jabez and Hannah, Feb. 26, 1754.
Reuben, s. Jabez and Hannah, Oct. 23, 1756.
Rhoda, d. Jabez and Hannah, Feb. 23, 1770.
Roxy M. [ch. Royall and Roxy B.], May 15, 1830.
Sarah, d. Jabez and Hannah, Jan. 13, 1762.
———, s. Jabez and Hannah, July 9, 1752.

RYAN, Thomas, d. Thomas F. (b. Cambridge) and Elizabeth (b. Salem), Apr. 18, 1849.

SAGE, Mary, d. Samuel and Lucy, May 19, 1816.
Samuel, s. Sam[ue]l and Lucy, Apr. 8, 1818.
Samuel, s. Samuel and Lucy, Sept. 28, 1826.

SALTMARSH, Deborah, d. Seth and Ruth, Mar. 19, 1776.
Ruth, d. Seth and Ruth, Mar. 29, 1774.
Thomas, s. Seth and Ruth, Aug. 29, 1772.

SHERMAN, Lydia, d. Rev. Nathaniel and Lydia, Sept. 9, 1765.
Nathaniel, s. Rev. Nathaniel and Lydia, Oct. 30, 1760.
Thaddeus, s. Rev. Nathaniel and Lydia, Mar. 24, 1763.

SIMONDS, Abigail, d. Benja[min] and Sarah, June 21, 1750.
Ammittai, d. Zebedee and Ammittai, Apr. 7, 1812.
Bethiah, d. Zebedee and Ammittai, July 23, 1821.
Caroline, d. Benjamin Jr. and Mary, Jan. 5, 1814.
Daniel, s. Lemuel and Polley, Jan. 17, 1801.
Edward, s. Zebedee and Ammitai, Jan. 29, 1819 [*sic*, see Harriet].
Eliza Ann, d. John and Ann, Aug. 1, 1826.
George, s. Zebedee and Ammittai, Jan. 15, 1810.
Harriet, d. Zebedee and Ammitai, Nov. 6, 1818 [*sic*, see Edward].
Henry, s. Zebedee and Ammitai, Jan. 9, 1817.

SIMONDS, Jane, d. Benj[ami]n Jr. and Elizabeth, July 17, 1819.
John Webber, s. Zebedee and Ammithai, Jan. 14, 1808.
Justin, s. Benjamin Jr. and Elizabeth, Jan. 6, 1824.
Laura Ann, d. George and Ann, July 10, 1842.
Mary Ann, d. Benjamin Jr. and Mary, Nov. 22, 1815.
Minerva, d. Benjamin Jr. and Elizabeth, May 21, 1821.
Rebakah, d. Benjamin and Sarah, May 17, 1745.
Sarah, d. Benjamin and Sarah, Sept. 9, 1747.
William, s. Zebedee and Ammitai, Apr. 2, 1814.
William Porter, s. Moses and Martha, Aug. 3, 1829.
Zebedee, " Posthumos " s. Dea. Zebdee and Ammittai, May 10, 1827.

SKELTON, Artemas, s. Daze and Keziah, May 21, 1794.
Edwin, s. Elijah and Sarah, Sept. 28, 1820.
Elijah, s. Capt. Elijah and Sarah, Mar. 27, 1816.
Emily, d. Elijah and Sarah, Aug. 7, 1822.
Emily, d. Elijah and Sarah, July 4, 1823.
Horace, s. Daze and Keziah, Nov. 21, 1793, in Woburn.
Lendel, s. Daze and Keziah, Oct. 6, 1795.
Lendell, twin s. Daze and Keziah, July 30, 1797.
Lowell, twin s. Daze and Keziah, July 30, 1797.
Mary Louisa, d. Elias and Louisa, Oct. 5, 1833.
Samuel, s. Elias and Louisa, June 20, 1832.
Sarah, d. Elijah and Sarah, Oct. 31, 1818.
William, s. Elijah and Sarah, Jan. 16, 1826.

SMITH, John Loring, s. Loring and Isabella, Jan. 1, 1847.

SPALDING, Augustus, s. Charles and Elizabeth, July 18, 1833.
Caroline Augusta, d. Charles and Elizabeth, Jan. 13, 1839.
George, s. Charles and Elizabeth, Dec. 17, 1831.
Lewis, s. Charles and Elizabeth C., June 10, 1828.

SPRAGUE (see Sprake), Susannah, d. Lt. John (Sprauge) and Phebe, July 11, 1798.

SPRAKE (see Sprague), Elizabeth, d. Lt. John and Phebe, Jan. 1, 1793.
Joel, s. Lt. John and Phebe, Mar. 15, 1791.
John, s. John and Phebe, Oct. 15, 1788.
Mary, d. Lt. John and Phebe, Oct. 15, 1795.
Phebe, d. John and Phebe, Aug. 14, 1784.
Sarah, d. John and Phebe, July 10, 1787.

STAPLES, Henry Oliver, s. Henry H. and Catherine, Feb. 18, 1848.

STARNS (see Stearns, Sterns), Nathan, s. Zacheriah and Sarah, Apr. 27, 1737.

STEARNS (see Starns, Sterns), Abigail, w. Rev. Samuel, d. Rev. Samuel French of Andover, May 29, 1776. G.R.
Abigail French, d. Rev. Samuel and Abigail, Aug. 18, 1798.
Abigail French, d. Rev. Samuel and Abigail, Jan. 17, 1800.
Abner, s. Edward and Lucy, July 9, 1766.
Allise, d. Edward and Lucy, Aug. 13, 1764.
Ann Catherine, d. Rev. Samuel and Abigail, Oct. 10, 1816.
Charles Blucher, s. W[illia]m and Betsey, Aug. 16, 1814.
Charlotte Esther, d. Rev. Samuel and Abigail, Sept. 17, 1814.
Daniel, s. Zachariah and Sarah, May 19, 1732.
Ebenezer Sperry, s. Rev. Samuel and Abigaiil, Dec. 23, 1819.
Edward, s. Edward and Lucy, Jan. 10, 1761.
Edward, s. Edward and Lucy, June 25, 1768.
Edward, s. Elijah and Elizabeth, Dec. 13, 1804.
Edward Josiah, s. Elijah and Elizabeth, Feb. 17, 1806.
Edward Josiah, s. Elijah Esq. and Elizabeth, Feb. 24, 1810.
Elijah, s. Edward and Lucy, May 2, 1770.
Elijah Wyman, s. Elijah and Elizabeth, Jan. 8, 1813.
Elizabeth Caroline, d. W[illia]m and Betsey, Dec. 9, 1811.
Elizabeth Williams, d. Rev. Samuel and Abigail, July 29, 1810.
Ellbridge Wyman, s. Simion and Sally, Apr. 22, 1803.
Emily Ann, d. W[illia]m and Clarissa, Oct. 28, 1838.
Frederick, s. William A. and Clarissa, Mar. 19, 1846.
George, s. Elijah and Elizabeth, Aug. 30, 1815.
George Washington, twin s. Rev. Samuel and Abigail, Sept. 1, 1812.
Henry Augustus, s. William A. and Clarissa, Feb. 26, 1836.
Horatio Davis, s. William and Betsey, Jan. 19, 1803.
Isaac Davis, s. W[illia]m and Betsey, July 21, 1821.
John, s. Zacheriah (Starns) and Sarah, Feb. 17, 1728.
Jonathan French, s. Rev. Samuel and Abigail, Sept. 4, 1808.
Josiah Atherton, twin s. Rev. Samuel and Abigail, Sept. 1, 1812.
Josiah Obed, s. Obed and Mahitable, Oct. 17, 1830.
Leonard, s. Leonard and Sarah, May 25, 1812.
Lucy, d. Edward and Lucy, Mar. 24, 1756.
Lucy Minerva, d. Simion and Sally, Sept. 6, 1805.
Mary Elizabeth, d. Elijah and Elizabeth, Oct. 31, 1807.
Mary Holyoke, d. Rev. Samuel and Abigail, Nov. 14, 1806.
Matilda Caroline, d. W[illia]m and Betsey, May 9, 1806.
Rachel, d. Edward and Lucy, Nov. 3, 1758.
Sally Miranda, d. Simion and Sally, May 12, 1808.

STEARNS, Samuel, Rev., ———, 1770, in Epping, N.H. G.R.
Samuel French, s. Elijah and Elizabeth, Apr. 25, 1818.
Samuel Horatio, s. Rev. Samuel and Abigail, Sept. 12, 1801.
Samuel Wirt, s. W[illia]m A. and Clarissa, Sept. 28, 1841.
Sarah, d. Zachria (Sterns) and Sarah, Aug. 9, 1734.
Sarah Caroline, d. Rev. Samuel and Abigail, Apr. 15, 1803.
Selinda, d. William and Betsey, Sept. 18, 1804.
Simeon, s. Edward and Lucy, Apr. 17, 1772.
Solomon, s. Edward and Lucy, May 12, 1757.
Susanna, d. Edward and Lucy, Dec. 19, 1762.
William Albert, s. W[illia]m and Betsey, Oct. 12, 1809.
William Augustus, s. Rev. Samuel and Abigail, Mar. 17, 1805.
William F., s. W[illiam] A. and Clarissa, Mar. 19, 1846.

STERNS (see Starns, Stearns), Zachriah, s. Zachriah and Sarah, Feb. 11, 1729–30.

STEVENS, Lorenzo, s. Lorenzo and Mary G. P., Dec. 26, 1846.

STILES, Charles Frederick, s. Francis and Eliza, July 24, 1842.
Lewis Cars, s. Francis and Elvira, Dec. 29, 1845.
Maria Eliza, d. Francis and Eliza, Aug. 2, 1844.
Mary Elizabeth, d. Francis and Eliza, June 28, 1843.

SWAIN, Hannah Malvina, d. Warren and Hannah, July 8, 1821.

SWEETSER, Thomas Thaxter, s. Adaniriam G. and Mary, June 6, 1836.

TAYLER (see Taylor), Hephzibah, d. David and Ruth, July 30, 1748.

TAYLOR (see Tayler), David, s. David and Hannah, July 5, 1727.
David, s. David and Hannah, Dec. 20, 1739.
David, s. Jonathan and Mary, Apr. 23, 1757.
Elezar, s. David and Hannah, Apr. 12, 1734.
Elizabeth, d. David (Tayler) and Hannah, Feb. 1, 17[ ] [rec. between Jan. 29, 1741, and Sept. 5, 1744].
Hannah, d. David (Talor) and Hanna, May 28, 1725.
Jonathan, s. David and Hannah, Feb. 27, 1729–30.
Jonathan, s. Jonath[an] and Mary, May 29, 1755.
Lucy, d. Jonathan and Mary, June 15, 1762.
Lydia, d. David and Hannah, Mar. 17, 1738.
Lydia, d. Jonathan and Mary, July 24, 1766.
Mary, d. David and Hannah, Feb. 20, 1731–2.
Mary, d. Jonathan and Mary, Oct. 3, 1759.

BEDFORD BIRTHS. 53

TAYLOR, Nathan, s. David and Hannah, Jan. 29, 1741.
Sarah, d. David and Hannah, May 27, 1736.
Sarah, d. Jonathan and Mary, Feb. 19, 1764.
Susey, d. David and R., May 6, 17[ ] [rec. between Sept. 5, 1744, and July 30, 1748].

THURSTON, Lucinda, d. Stephen and Philomela, July 21, 1804.

TRASK, Daniel, s. Joseph and Eunice, Oct. 7, 1797.
Oliver, s. Joseph and Eunice, June 3, 1794.
Peter, s. Joseph and Eunice, Aug. 4, 1792.

TWISS, James Franklin, s. Daniel (b. Nottingham, West N. H.) and Eleanor (b. New Brunswick), Oct. 28, 1848.

WALTAN, Joshua, s. Joshua and Hannah, Oct. 9, 1770.

WATTS, Angelina Pratt, d. Nathaniel P. and Ann M., July 30, 1844.
Jane Damon, d. Isaac (b. Malden) and Martha C., Aug. 17, 1848.

WEBBER, Asa, s. John and Sarah, June 20, 1775.
Benj[ami]n, s. John and Sarah, Dec. 21, 1770.
Benjamin Abbott, s. William and Mary, Dec. 25, 1802.
Betsey Abbott, d. William and Mary, Aug. 26, 1806.
Caroline Matilda Abbott [dup. (Wibber) omits Abbott], d. Benjamin A. [dup. omits A.] and Mary Ann, Apr. 23, 1827.
Charles Stone, s. Joseph Jr. and Eliza, Nov. 17, 1820.
Charles Warren, s. William and Mary W., Sept. 11, 1836.
Elbert Franklin, s. William and Mary W., Dec. 6, 1842.
Eliot, d. Asa and Eliot Reed, June 26, 1804.
Fidelia Page, d. Hiram and Fidelia, Feb. 25, 1834, in S. Boston.
George Edward, s. Hiram and Phidelia, Jan. 24, 1827, in Billerica.
Hannah Rebeckah, d. James and Hannah, Sept. 16, 1810.
Hiram, s. William and Mary, June 9, 1794.
James, s. John and Sarah, Oct. 16, 1772.
Job, s. John and Sarah, May 16, 1769.
John, s. John and Sarah, Dec. 31, 1760.
John Lane, s. Asa and Eliot Reed, Dec. 3, 1808.
Joseph, s. John and Sarah, Nov. 21, 1764.
Levi William Freeman, s. Benja[min] A. and Mary Ann, Feb. 17, 1832.
Lucy, twin d. Capt. John and Sarah, Oct. 27, 1780.
Lucy, twin d. Asa and Eliot, June 5, 1811.

WEBBER, Lydia, twin d. Capt. John and Sarah, Oct. 27, 1780.
Lydia, twin d. Asa and Eliot, June 5, 1811.
Lydia Page, d. James and Hannah, Jan. 27, 1813.
Marcus Bruce, s. Artemas and Sarah W., Mar. 9, 1828.
Maria Cordelia, d. Artemas and Sarah, Dec. 4, 1837.
Mary, d. William and Mary, Feb. 22, 1799.
Mary Abbott, d. Hiram and Phidelia, July 16, 1825.
Moses, s. William and Mary, June 27, 1811.
Octa, s. Joseph Jr. and Eliza, July 14, 1819.
Polley, d. William and Mary, May 24, 1792.
Ruhamah, d. Asa and Eliot Reed, Apr. 14, 1802.
Ruth Adelaide, d. Artemas and Sarah W., Feb. 16, 1834.
Sarah, d. John and Sarah, Mar. 18, 1766.
Sarah Abagail, d. Artemas and Sarah W., Jan. 23, 1830.
Susana, d. John and Sarah, Jan. 28, 1774.
Susanna, d. William and Mary, Nov. 14, 1809.
Thomas, s. John and Sarah, Dec. 27, 1777.
William, s. John and Sarah, Nov. 29, 1762.
William, s. William and Mary, May 19, 1796.
William Augustus, s. William and Mary W., June 27, 1840.

WHEELER (see Whellor, Whelor), Hannah, d. John and Hannah, Mar. 22, 1758.
John, s. John and Hannah, Dec. 27, 1755.
John, s. John and Byer, Sept. 9, 1783.
Richard, s. John and Hannah, May 17, 1760.
Salley, d. John and Byer, Sept. 12, 1781, in Berry.

WHELLOR (see Wheeler, Whelor), Thaddeus, s. James (Whelor) and Mary, Dec. 16, 1742.

WHELOR (see Wheeler, Whellor), Abigal, d. Peetter and Hannah, Mar. 25, 1735–6.
Benjamin, s. Peter and Hannah, Aug. 22, 1739.
Daniel, s. James and Mary, Apr. 23, 1736.
Elizabeth, d. James and Mary, Mar. 23, 1734.
Hanah, d. Peter and Hannah, Oct. 7, 1733.
James, s. James and Mary, May 16, 1731.
Love, d. Peter (Wheor) and Hanna, May 10, 1728.
Martha, d. Joseph and Ruth, Sept. 24, 1730.
Petter, s. Petter and Hannah, Jan. 17, 1730–1.
Richard, s. Richard and Gemima, Oct. 14, 1730.
Zeubee, d. James and Mary, Oct. 29, 1738.

WHETIKAR (see Whitaker, Whiteker, Whitiker), Samuel, s.

Samuel (Whetickar) and Abigol [Tabitha, written above], Sept. 15, 1735.

WHETNE (see Whettnee), Jonathan, s. Zacheus and Mary, Jan. 12, 1736–7.

Zacheus, s. Zacheus and Mary, Mar. 15, 1734–5.

WHETTNEE (see Whetne), Shadrach, s. Zacckeus (Whetnee) and Mary, May 17, 1739.

WHIPPEL, Timothy, s. John and Susana, Nov. 26, 1727.

WHIT (see White), Dorcas, d. Nathan and Dorcas, Nov. 15, 1790.

Eliza Ann, d. Albert and Dorothy, Dec. 20, 1834.

Samuel Lane, s. Nathan and Dorcas, Dec. 23, 1792.

WHITAKER (see Whetikar, Whiteker, Whitiker), Bettey, d. Samuel and Tabitha, Aug. 11, 1748.

Lydia, d. Samuel and Tabitha, June 19, 1746.

Tabitha, d. Sam[ue]ll and Tabitha, Apr. 14, 1754, in Concord.

William, s. Samuel and Tabitha, July 28, 1750, in Concord.

WHITCOMB, Emma Frances, d. Merrill and Hannah, Nov. 19 [1844], in Boxboro.

WHITE (see Whit), Betsey, d. Nathan and Dorcas, July 19, 1788.

Eben, s. Albert and Dorothy, July 10, 1832.

Jane, d. Albert and Dorothy, Oct. 27, 1836.

———, twin s. Nathan and Dorcas, July 22, 1789.

———, twin s. Nathan and Dorcas, July 22, 1789.

WHITEKER (see Whetikar, Whitaker, Whitiker), Eliza. Samuel and Tabitha, July 22, 1742.

Lucy, d. Samuel (Wheteker) and Tabitha, May 10, 1744.

WHITFORD, Ellen Frances, d. Hiram and Bethiah, June 1, 1844.

Harriet Augusta, d. Hiram and Bethiah, Feb. 20, 1843.

WHITIKER (see Whetikar, Whitaker, Whiteker), Hannah, d. Samuel (Wheteker) and Tabitha, Oct. 30, 1737.

WHITING, Mary, d. John and Anna, July 2, 1757.

WHITMOR (see Whitmore), Lucy, d. John and Martha, Nov. 8, 1745.

WHITMORE (see Whitmor), Ebenezar, s. John (Whitmoor) and Martha, Jan. 1, 1740–1.
John, s. John and Martha, Oct. 23, 1737.
John, s. John dec'd and Martha, June 13, 1749.
Martha, d. John (Whitmor) and Martha, Sept. 30, 1742.
Mary, d. John (Whitmor) and Martha, May 2, 1744.
Susanna, d. John and Martha, July 16, 1747.
William, s. John and Martha, Mar. 17, 1738–9.

WHITNEY (see Whetne, Whettnee).

WHITTEMORE, Elizabeth, d. Nathaniel and Jemima, July 20, 1758.

WILKINS, Ann Catherine, d. Silas and Catherine, Feb. 28, 1837.
Eliab Lane, s. Silas and Catherine, May 19, 1833.
George Everett, s. Silas and Catherine, Aug. 1, 1831.
Silas Granville, s. Silas and Catherine, Mar. 9, 1835.

WILLIS, Josiah H., s. Josiah H. and Lydia, Nov. 11, 1827.
Lydia Augusty, d. Josiah H. and Lydia, June 17, 1825.

WILLSON (see Wilson), Dolley E., d. James Jr. and Dolley, Feb. 20, 1809.
Elizabeth, d. Joseph and Elizabeth, Jan. 10, 1745–6.
Elizabeth, d. Francis and Elizabeth, Sept. 27, 1807.
Elmira C., d. James Jr. and Dolley, Sept. 18, 1811.
Francis, s. James and Abi, Mar. 15, 1781.
Francis, s. Francis and Elizabeth, Dec. 16, 1804.
George, twin ch. James Jr. and Dolley, Apr. 28, 1807.
Jacob, s. Jacob and Hanna, Sept. 19, 1734.
James, s. James and Lydia, Dec. 14, 1752.
James, s. James and Abie, Nov. 14, 1775.
James, s. James Jr. and Dolley, Sept. 3, 1804.
Jonathan, s. Joseph and Eliz[abet]h, Nov. 15, 1756.
Lydia, d. James and Lydia, Apr. 22, 1744.
Mary, d. James and Lydia, June 17, 1748.
Mary Ann, twin ch. James Jr. and Dolley, Apr. 28, 1807.
Pattee, d. James and Lydia, Aug. 30, 1750.
Rebecka, d. Frances [*sic*] and Patience, May 7, 1733.
Rhoda, d. Joseph and Elizabeth, Nov. 28 [blotted], 1753.
Rhoda, d. Joseph and Eliz[abet]h, Jan. 2, 1759.
Ruth, d. James and Lydia, Oct. 6, 1745.
Ruth, d. Joseph and Elizabeth, Aug. 30, 1748.
Samuel, s. Joseph and Elizabeth, Oct. 7, 1750.

WILLSON, Sarah, d. Joseph and Elizabeth, Feb. 22, 1746-7.
Thaddeus, s. James and Abi, Nov. 16, 1778.

WILSON (see Willson), Abigal, d. Samuel and Sarah, Mar. 12, 1730-1.
Ellen Frances, d. Willard and Elizabeth Wallace, Dec. 21, 1842.
Francis Ware, s. Willard and Elizabeth G., Jan. 9, 1848.
Frederick Llewellyn, s. Willard and Elizabeth, Apr. 8, 1837.
Ida, d. Willard and Elizabath G., July 27, 1846.
James [dup. Willson], s. James Jr. and Dolly [dup. Dolley], Jan. 21, 1801.
Nellie Susan, d. Francis and Elvira, Mar. 9, 1845.
Timothy, s. Samuel and Sarah, Sept. 4, 1728.
Wallace, s. Willard and Elizabeth, Nov. 17 [1844].

WINSHIP, Naby, d. Richard and Sally, Feb. 14, 1790.
Neamiah, s. Richard and Salley, Apr. 4, 1792.
Salley, d. Richard and Sally, Aug. 9, 1788.

WOLCUT, Ann Eliza, d. Rev. Robert F. and Mary, June 1, 1835.

WOODS, Henry, Oct. 27, 1834.

WOODWARD, Allice, d. Rev. George W. and w., Feb. 1, 1844.

WOOLLEY, Asa, s. Nathan and Sarah, July 11, 1761, in Hollis.
Esther, d. Nathan and Sarah, June 1, 1759.
Eunice, d. John and Mary, Jan. 15, 1756.
Hannah, d. John and Mary, July 7, 1760.
John, s. Thomas [and] Marrah, Nov. 30, 1729.
John, s. John and Mary, Aug. 16, 1754.
John, s. John and Mary, Apr. 19, 1757.
Jonathan, s. John and Mary, Aug. 22, 1758.
Nathan, s. Thomas and Marrah, Dec. 3, 1733.
Nathan, s. Nathan and Sarah, July 20, 1757.
Sarah, d. Thomas and Marah, July 17, 1737.
Thomas, s. John and Mary, Mar. 14, 1763, in Monson.

WRIGHT, Betsey, d. Dea. James and Ruth, Aug. 6, 1789.
Betsey, d. James Jr. and Dorcas, Mar. 28, 1810.
Bettey, d. Judah and Tabitha, Jan. 11, 1770.
Caroline, d. James Jr. and Dorcas, Sept. 28, 1814.
Dorcas Emily, d. James Jr. and Dorcas, July 12, 1806.
George Cleavland, s. Joel and Dolly H., Jan. 7, 1823.
Hannah, d. John Tidd and Hannah, Mar. 18, 1797.
James, s. James and Ruth, Nov. 2, 1774.
Joel Edward, s. Joel and Dolley H., Feb. 25, 1821.

WRIGHT, John Tidd, s. James and Ruth, Dec. 16, 1777.
Joseph Bigsbe, s. James Jr. and Dorcas, Sept. 13, 1804.
Margaret Sophronia, d. James Jr. and Dorcas, Feb. 8, 1812.
Patty, d. Judah and Tabitha, Feb. 1, 1772.
Ruth, d. James and Ruth, Aug. 9, 1769.
Sally, d. James and Ruth, Dec. 12, 1771.
Sally, d. James and Dorcas, Sept. 22, 1808.
Tabitha, d. Judah and Tabitha, Feb. 25, 1768.
Timothy Page, s. James Jr. and Dorcas, Jan. 25, 1800.
———, ch. James Jr., Oct. 17, 1797. C.R.

WYLLIS (see Willis).

WYMAN, Isaac, s. Nath[anie]l Jr. and Betsey, Dec. 29, 1796.
Samuel Thompson [dup. T.], s. Samuel and Sarah, May 12, 1845.

NEGROES, ETC.

Peter, "a Revolutionary soldier, freed slave of Rev. Josiah Stearns, Epping, N.H., faithful hired servant of Rev. Samuel Stearns," ———, 1750. G.R.

BEDFORD MARRIAGES.

BEDFORD MARRIAGES.

To the year 1850.

ABBOT (see Abbott), Allice and Simon Davis, June 3, 1806.
Mary and Daniel Parker, Aug. 4, 1774.
Mary and William Webber, May 10, 1791.
Moses Jr. and Alise [Alice, M.R.] Stearns, Dec. 7, 1786.

ABBOTT (see Abbot), Allice and Stephen Lane, May 1, 1806. [Abbot, C.R.]
Bette and Oliver Reed Jr., May 18, 1786. [Betty Abbot, M.R.]
Elizabeth and Abijah Cutler, Dec. 9, 1756. [Elisabeth Abbot, M.R.]
Hannah of Andover, and John Lane, Mar. 16, 1732, in Andover.
Lucy S. and Timothy Kinsman, Mar. 16, 1809.
Moses and Mary Hill, Apr. 15, 1755, in Charlestown.
Oliver R. and Mary Ann Wilson, Nov. 17, 1825.
Oliver R. and Mary Ann Buttrick, June 24, 1827.
Ruth E., Mrs., and Augustus Pierce, Nov. 15, 1835.
S. Caroline and Seth H. Austin, Feb. 13, 1842.
Sarah and Isaac Stearns, Feb. 11, 1747–8. [Abbot, M.R.]

ADAMS, Abel B., Dr., and Susan Merriam, Apr. 25, 1841.
Nathaniel [Nathanael, C.R.] of Worcester, and Mrs. Martha Whitmore, Dec. 10, 1751.

ALLEN (see Alline), Reuben and Rusa Fairbanks, June 4, 1795, in Dedham.
Sally and Benjamin Parker, June 28, 1801.

ALLINE (see Allen), Rebeckah and Franklin Butters, Nov. 17, 1819.

ATCHERSON, James S., 28, of Waltham, s. Tho[ma]s and Charlotte of Rockingham, Vt., and Clariot P. Munroe, July 26, 1848.

ATKINS, Thomas G., 58, b. Boston, of Boston, s. Gibbs and Hannah of Boston, and Mary M. Tuttle, wid., Oct. 12, 1848.

AUSTIN, Seth H. and S. Caroline Abbott, Feb. 13, 1842.

BACHELDER, Desire and Joseph Brown, Nov. 6, 1754, in Woburn.
Jemima of Beverly, and Joseph Hartwell, Dec. 12, 1750, in Beverly.

BACON, Abigail and James Simonds, July 26, 1739.
Abigail and William Ripley 3d, Mar. 14, 1833.
Abijah and Rhoda Bacon, Feb. 29, 1776. M.R.
Albert and Susan Reed, June 2, 1825.
Amittai and Benjamin Bacon Jr., Dec. 31, 1789.
Benjamin and Katharine Lane, Feb. 15, 1738–9.
Benjamin Jr. and Esther Davis, May 27, 1766.
Benjamin Jr. and Amittai Bacon, Dec. 31, 1789.
Benjamin 3d and Sylvania Lane, Apr. 7, 1822.
Caroline and Isaac W. Hurd, May 14, 1837.
Caroline, 37, d. Stephen and Mary, and Abel S. Monroe, widr., Nov. 28 [1844.]
David and Lucretia Simonds, Jan. 3, 1771, in Lexington.
Edward and Charlotte Hatch, Nov. 28, 1839.
Elbridge and Louisa Reed, Apr. 27, 1823.
Elijah and Amittai Lane, ———, 1785. [Amity, Dec. 15, M.R.]
Elijah and Mary Watson, Jan. 26, 1823.
Elisabeth and Jonathan Willson, Oct. 8, 1761. M.R.
Eliza and Joseph Webber Jr., Jan. 10, 1819.
Eliza Ann and Prescott J. Bigelow, Apr. 16, 1840.
Elizabeth and Ebenezer Richardson, May 21, 1733, in Billerica.
Elizabeth and Daniel Robinson, June 4, 1794.
Elizabeth and Nathaniel Wyman Jr., Apr. 9, 1795, in Lexington.
Eunice and Samuel Bacon, Mar. 30, 1747–8. [Mar. 10, C.R. M.R.]
Flag and Polly Blodget, Jan. 8, 1792. [Flagg, M.R.]
Flagg, Capt., and Sarah Blodgett, Sept. 21, 1800. [Flag, C.R.]
Isaac P. and Susanna E. Buttrick, May 3, 1831.
Iza and Dr. Benjamin Skelton, Oct. 18, 1810.
Jacob of Lexington, and Katherine Davis, Feb. 13, 1768, in Lexington.
John and Elizabeth Starns, Dec. 20, 1744. [Stearns, C.R.]
John and Hannah Lane, May 6, 1779.
Jonas and Betty Smith, May 18, 1784, in Lexington.
Jonathan and Elizabeth Wyman, Sept. 22, 1739, in Woburn.
Jonathan and Abigail Clark, July 15, 1806.
Lucy and Joseph Adams Wellington, Mar. 25, 1798. [Wellington, C.R.]

BACON, Lydia and Amos Brooks, Feb. 6, 1745-6.
Maria L., 22, d. Elbridge and Louisa, and Joel Mansfield, Mar. 4, 1847.
Martha and Aaron Priest, May 7, 1782. M.R.
Martha and Joseph Hosmer, Oct. 1, 1837.
Mary and Nathan Priest, July 5, 1780, in Bolton.
Mary E., 22, of Lowell, d. Elijah and Mary, and Coates Bulfinch, June 14, 1846.
Mical and Sarah Whittemore, Nov. 24, 1743. [Michael and Sarah Whittermore, C.R.]
Michael and Elizebeth [Elizabeth, C.R.] Lane, Mar. 5, 1746-7. [Elisabeth, M.R.]
Nabby and John Richardson, June 2, 1794, in Billerica.
Nancy and Cyrus Warren, Dec. 16, 1819.
Nancy and John A. Merriam, Apr. 14, 1830.
Patty and James Davis, Nov. 27, 1823.
Polley and Jessee Dean, Mar. 7, 1811.
Reuben and Sarah Clark, Jan. 15, 1807. [Jan. 18, C.R.]
Reuben Jr. and Ruth Corbin, June 30, 1832.
Rhoda and Abijah Bacon, Feb. 29, 1776. M.R.
Ruth and Joseph Robbins, Apr. 18, 1751.
Sally and William Gleason Jr., Feb. 11, 1795, in Billerica.
Samuel of Stow, and Eunice Bacon, Mar. 30, 1747-8. [Mar. 10, C.R. M.R.]
Sarah and Jothom Wheelor, Mar. 30, 1775. [Jonathan Wheeler, M.R.]
Sarah and William Whitford, Feb. 16, 1826.
Sarah and Edward Flint, Apr. 21, 1831.
Stephen and Mary Porter, Nov. 28, 1799.
Susanna and Nathan Brooks, Feb. 9, 1736-7. [Feb. 10, C.R.]
Susanna and Nathan Meril, Jan. 21, 1788. [Morril, M.R.]
Thomas and Elizabeth [Elisabeth, M.R.] Ditson, Apr. 11, 1749.
Thompson and Martha Hosmer, Oct. 16, 1783.
Thompson Jr. and Rebecca P. Porter, Apr. 17, 1821.
Warren and Lucy Ann Lawrence, Aug. 1, 1841.

BAILEY, Mary and Daniel H. [dup. omits H.] Butters, June 28, 1842.

BALCH, Joanna and Jesse Templeton, Nov. 20, 1825.

BALL, Abner of Concord, and Mary Reed, Apr. 30, 1789.
Acsak of Springfield, and Daniel Rose, June 25, 1747, in Springfield.

BALL, Gardner of Boston, and Mary Vila Shaffer, June 30, 1825.
Samuel of Concord, and Rebekah Jones, Nov. 4, 1784.

BANNON, John of Lexington, and Sarah Mason, Sept. 25, 1843.

BARRAN, Benjamin of Concord, and Sarah Blood, Nov. 13, 1783. [Barron, M.R.]

BARRAR, Salle and Reuben Reed, Aug. 28, 1782. [Sally Barrer, M.R.]

BARRETT, Polley and Nathan Stow, May 12, 1814.

BARRON (see Barran).

BATCHELDER (see Bachelder).

BATEMAN, Anne, Mrs., of Concord, and Richard Wheeler, Dec. 10, 1760.
Hepsibah and Nathaniel Reed, Jan. 16, 1772, in Lexington.
Lydia and Stephen Davis Jr., Nov. 6, 1766.

BATES, Adolphus of Stow, and Mrs. Lavinia Bates, Nov. 14, 1839.
Lavinia, Mrs., and Adolphus Bates, Nov. 14, 1839.

BATHRICK, Samuel of Concord, and Susanna Yours, Dec. 11, 1740. C.R.

BEAN, Nicholas M. and Belinda Miller, Oct. 13, 1842.

BEARD, Josiah of Billerica, and Sarah Page, Dec. 29, 1784.

BELLAMY, Esther and William Merriam, Nov. 30, 1769.

BEMIS, Jacob of Waltham, and Hepsibah Phillips, Nov. 26, 1788, in Waltham.

BENNER, Margaret of Billerica, and James Ingles, Mar. 13, 1788 [?], in Billerica.

BIGELOW, Prescott J. of Abington, and Eliza Ann Bacon, Apr. 16, 1840.

BINGHAN, Lucretia of Carlisle, and Moses Hayward, Apr. 30, 1829.

BLANCHARD, Isaac of Charlestown, and Caroline Gragg, Oct. 27, 1840.

BLINN, Harriet, Mrs., and Oliver W. Lane, Feb. 26, 1843.

BLODGET (see Blodgett), Jonathan and Molley [Molly, M.R.] Fitch, Jan. 12, 1757.
Polly and Flag [Flagg, M.R.] Bacon, Jan. 8, 1792.

BLODGETT (see Blodget), Sarah and Capt. Flagg [Flag, C.R.] Bacon, Sept. 21, 1800.
Simeon and Sally Fitch, Oct. 25, 1804.

BLOOD, Francis, Mrs., of Carlisle, and Samuel Lane, May 21, 1799, in Carlisle.
Mary of Concord, and John Woolley, Apr. 30, 1754. [Wooley, M.R.]
Sarah and Benjamin Barran, Nov. 13, 1783. [Barron, M.R.]

BOND, Joshua of Concord, and Martha Lane, June 12, 1775. [Jan. 12, M.R.]

BOWEN, John R., widr., 34, of Charlestown, s. Benjamin and w., and Harriett H. Dean, Feb. 11, 1845.

BOWERS, Bradley of Billerica, and Lydia Moor, Feb. 19, 1793.
Bradley Varnum and Martha Porter, Aug. 24, 1817.

BOWES, Lucy, Mrs., and Rev. Samuel Cook, Nov. 28, 1762. [Nov. 25, M.R.]

BOWMAN, Abigail and Rodulphus Comer, May 18, 1763, in Lexington.
Francis and Sarah Simonds, June 24, 1756, in Lexington.
Hannah and Abraham Meriam, Apr. 6, 1778.
Hannah [and] William Goodrich, July 2, 1791, in Concord.
John and Hannah Frye, Sept. 19, 1781, in Andover.
Nathan and Esther French, May 30, 1771. [Nathaniel, M.R.]
Ruth of Lexington, and John Lane Jr., Feb. 13, 1745-6.
Sarah and William Maxwel, Nov. 23, 1773. [Maxwell, Nov. 23, 1775, M.R.]

BOYD, Samuel of Boston, and Eleanor McIllvane, Nov. 21, 1745. [Nov. 18, C.R.]

BRIDGE, Samuel of Lexinton, and Susan Page, Apr. 9, 1734. [Samuel of Lexington, and Susanna Paige, C.R.]

BRIGGS, George and Mary W. Lane, Sept. 26, 1841.

BROCKWAY, William and Ann Hosmer, Dec. 1, 1808.

BROOKS, Amos of Harvard, and Lydia Bacon, Feb. 6, 1745-6.
Hannah of Lincoln, and John Meriam Jr., Dec. 4, 1760.
Nathan of Concord, and Susanna Bacon, Feb. 9, 1736-7. [Feb. 10, C.R.]

BROWN, Abraham of Brookline, and Desire Porter, Sept. 21, 1774, in Concord.
Anna and Josiah Ireland, Aug. 22, 1770, in Lexington.
Bowman of Lexington, and Abigail Page, Feb. 7, 1765.
Desire and Stephen Meeds, Feb. 5, 1765. [Mead, M.R.]
Desire and Samuel Hartwell, Oct. 26, 1779.
Edward Sheaf and Betsey Winchester Flint, Sept. 11, 1799, in Dracutt.
Elizabeth of Concord, and Stephen Daves Jr., Sept. 2, 1736. [Davis, C.R.]
Hannah and Andrew Evans, Feb. 12, 1784.
Hannah Elizabeth and Augustus R. Fuller, Sept. 23, 1833.
Jonas Jr. of Billerica, and Rebecca Durent, Mar. 3, 1839.
Joseph and Desire Bachelder, Nov. 6, 1754, in Woburn.
Joseph and Betsey Wright, Oct. 5, 1809.
Joseph and Rachel Fitch, Feb. 18, 1819.
Josiah D., 35, of Shirley, and Catherine Tarbell, Apr. 10 [1845].
Lucy of Lexington, and Joseph Converse Jr., Sept. 15, 1788, in Lexington.
Lydia of Billerica, and Valintine P. Rollins, Apr. 6, 1837.
Moses F., 21, s. Joseph and Rachel, and Elizabeth Smith, Aug. 25 [1844].
Nathaniel and Ruth Lane, Mar. 30, 1797.
Polley and Moses Fitch Jr., Dec. 6, 1810.
Sarah of Lexington, and Nathaniel Page Jr., Dec. 15, 1774, in Lexington.

BRYANT, Sally and John Russell, Mar. 30, 1835.

BUCK, Lydia and Zachariah Fitch, Aug. 4, 1763, in Groton.

BULFINCH, Coates, 24, of Lowell, s. Jeremiah, and Mary E. Bacon, June 14, 1846.

BURK, Michael and Mrs. Nancy McAuley, Dec. 3, 1839.

BURNAM, Louisa and Nathan Fitch, Sept. 9, 1834.
Mary An and Leonard White, Nov. 29, 1832.

BUTLER, Catherine D., 21, d. Dexter and Ruth, and Stephens Haynes Jr., Sept. 5, 1847.
Lucy and Lewis P. Gleason, Oct. 2, 1827.

BUTLER, Mary Ann, 22, d. Samuel and Mary, and John S. Ladd, Sept. 5, 1847.
Sophronia and Lewis P. Gleason, Mar. 3, 1826.

BUTTERFIELD, John and Elizabeth Hodgman, Sept. 24, 1840.

BUTTERS, Abel and Molley Marshall, May 24, 1812.
Daniel H. [dup. omits H.] and Mary Bailey, June 28, 1842.
Franklin of Wilmington, and Rebeckah Alline, Nov. 17, 1819.
Lydia [dup. adds S.], b. Burlington, of Burlington, and William D. Reed, Apr. 20, 1843.
Sarah, 23, d. Jona[than] and Lydia, and David Reed, Apr. 15, 1848.
Thomas G., 25, s. Daniel and Susan, and Ruth E. Pierce, wid., Sept. 9, 1846.

BUTTRICK, Esther and Ebenezer Hayward, Nov. 27, 1828.
John P. and Mary W. Fuller, June —, 1827.
Mary Ann and Oliver R. Abbott, June 24, 1827.
Susanna E. and Isaac P. Bacon, May 3, 1831.

CALDWELL, William and Edith Porter, July 2, 1780.

CAREY (see Cary), Elizabeth and Daniel B. Piper, Dec. 1, 1836.

CARY (see Carey), William and Dorothy Wood, May 24, 1755, in Concord.

CENTER, Abigail and Samuel Wayman, Dec. 22, 1774. [Wyman, M.R.]

CHAMBER (see Chambers), Margaret and James Clark, Nov. 17, 1734. [Chambers, Nov. 19, C.R.]

CHAMBERLAIN (see Chamberlin), Dorcas and Timothy Phelps, Oct. 28, 1823.
Lydia of Chelmsford, and Isaac Patten, Sept. 16, 1760, in Chelmsford.
Phinehas W. and Almira Hatch, May 12, 1831.

CHAMBERLIN (see Chamberlain), Phinehas and Dorkes Varnum, Feb. 21, 1797, in Chelmsford.

CHAMBERS (see Chamber), James and Margaret Rankins, May 13, 1742.
Martha and Samuel Crooks, Sept. 26, 1739. C.R.

CHANDLER, Rebecca of Concord, and Eleazer Davis, June 17, 1731, in Concord.

CLARK, Abigail and Jonathan Bacon, July 15, 1806.
Benjamin and Martha Hosmer, May 6, 1812.
Daniel and Caroline Gleason, Apr. 14, 1834.
David and Elizabeth Gleason, Oct. 21, 1834.
David of W. Cambridge, and Lydia P. Webber, Feb. 21, 1839.
Ebenezer and Polley [Polly, c.r.] Sampson, Sept. 15, 1805.
Hiram, 32, of Lexington, s. Thomas and Lydia of Middlesex, Vt., and Mary M. Lane, Feb. 4, 1847.
James of Londonberry, and Margaret Chamber, Nov. 17, 1734. [James of N. Londonberry, and Margaret Chambers, Nov. 19, c.r.]
James and Hannah Hodgman, May 28, 1818.
Jane and Casas Prescut, negroes, May 18, 1780.
Leander, 29, of New Ipswich, N.H., s. Benjamin and Nancy, and Laura Hosmer, June 29, 1845.
Lydia F. of Lexington, and Moses Felt, Apr. 29, 1816.
Mary and Stephen Corbin, Oct. 25, 1804.
Sarah and Reuben Bacon, Jan. 15, 1807. [Jan. 18, c.r.]
William and Susan Sprague, Apr. 24, 1832.

CLEMENT, Rodney and Betsey Reed, Apr. 28, 1835.

COAD, Mary and James Cary Jones, July 19, 1787.

COLBURN, Joseph and Hannah Reed, May 26, 1807.
Reback and Amos Davis, Oct. 21, 1740. [Rebecca Colbourn, c.r.]
William of Lincoln, and Nabby Reed, May 28, 1816.

COMER, Rodulphus of Bridgwater, and Abigail Bowman, May 18, 1763, in Lexington.

COMEY, William S., 24, of Westford, s. Asa and Charlotte, and Almira Hayden, Apr. 13, 1845.

CONANT, Levi [dup. of Harvard] and Abigail Davis, June 26, 1794, in Concord.

CONSTANTINE, David and Abigail Harrington, Aug. 5, 1838, in Burlington.

CONVASS (see Convasse, Convers, Converse), Sarah and Jeremiah Goldsmith, Dec. 30, 178[ ] [? 1788]. [Convers, Dec. 30, 1778, m.r.]

CONVASSE (see Convass, Convers, Converse), Zebulon of Ringe, and Sarah Merriam, May 8, 1773. [Converse of Rindge, and Sarah Meriam, m.r.]

CONVERS (see Convass, Convasse, Converse), William and Sarah Hunt, Nov. 13, 1800.

CONVERSE (see Convass, Convasse, Convers), Joseph and Elizabeth Davis, May 27, 1762, in Lexington.
Joseph Jr. and Lucy Brown, Sept. 15, 1788, in Lexington.

COOK, Catherine G. and Henry Hosmer, Apr 6, 1843.
Samuel, Rev., of Cambridge, and Mrs. Lucy Bowes, Nov. 28, 1762. [Nov. 25, M.R.]

COOLEY, Daniel and Rebecca Freeman, Aug. 8, 1745, in Westfield.

COOPER, Warren, Rev., of Pomfret, Conn., and Lucretia Crosby, June 3, 1840.
William H., widr., 35, b. Littleton, s. Jona[than] and Sarah of Littleton, and Rachel Johnson, Dec. 27, 1846.

CORBIN, Ruth of New Ipswich, N.H., and Reuben Bacon Jr., June 30, 1832.
Sarah and Samuel Wyman, Oct. 26, 1837.
Stephen and Mary Clark, Oct. 25, 1804.

COREY, Charles C. and Hannah A. Lane, Nov. 27, 1839.

COTTING (see Cutting), James C. and Susannah H. Stearns, Jan. 3, 1841.

CRAWFORD, Thomas and Caroline Hazelett, Jan. 1, 1839.

CROOKS, Samuel of Westfield, and Martha Chambers, Sept. 26, 1739. C.R.

CROSBY, Cyrus F., s. Michael and Lois Lane, Jan. 9, 1844.
Ephraim of Billerica, and Mary Merriam, Apr. 17, 1755, in Billerica.
Hannah of Billerica, and Luke Lane, Mar. 24, 1791, in Billerica.
Joseph of Amherst, and Esther Lane, Sept. 24, 1778.
Josiah and Sarah Fitch, Aug. 23, 1750.
Louisa and John Powers, Sept. 29, 1822.
Lucretia and Rev. Warren Cooper, June 3, 1840.
Margaret T., 18, d. Michael and Margaret, and Abner D. Farnum, Sept. 14, 1848.
Mary and Luther Eaton, Nov. 11, 1823.
Michael, Dea., and Lucy Swain, May 19, 1816, in Boston.
Rachel and Nathan Simonds, May 21, 1818.

CUMMINGS, Ebenezer of Woburn, and Jemime Hartwell, June 22, 1774. [Cumings, and Jemima Hartwell, M.R.]

CUTLER, Abijah of Brookfield, and Elizabeth Abbott, Dec. 9, 1756. [Elisabeth Abbot, M.R.]
Almira and Albert Fitch, Nov. 25 [1841].
Amos B. and Mary P. Lane, Apr. 16, 1833.
Eliza J. and William Goodwin, May 26, 1836.
Mary and Francis B. Goodridge, Feb. 9, 1832.
Nathaniel C. and Susan G. Lane, Mar. 10, 1831.
Nathan[ie]l C., widr., 40, b. Ashby, s. Thomas and Rebecca, and Catherine Wheeler, May 10, 1849.
Rebecca and William F. Frost, Mar. 15, 1842.
Solomon of Lexington, and Rebekah Page, Feb. 23, 1762, in Lexington.
Thomas C. and Maria Wood, Apr. 17, 1828.
Thomas C. and Lois Wheat, Apr. 14, 1840.

CUTOR, Mary of Cambridge, and Peter Fasset, Mar. 24, 1736–7. [Cutter, and Peter Fassett, C.R.]

CUTTING (see Cotting), Susannah, wid., 22, and Lorenzo Phelps, Sept. 5, 1847.

DANFORTH, Abigail of Billerica, and Jonas Gleason, Jan. 20, 1795, in Billerica.
Abigail Prince and David Reed, Apr. 23, 1812.
Benjamin and Sarah Parker, July 7, 1748.
John and Mary Wait, Mar. 24, 1763, in Lexington.
Lydia of Billerica, and Ziba Lane, Apr. 1, 1778, in Billerica.
Rebeckah of Billerica, and Ephraim Davis, Mar. 21, 1737, in Billerica.
Sally Pollard and Benjamin Reed, Apr. 17, 1817.
Thomas of Billerica, and Rebeckah Simonds, Sept. 19, 1734, in Billerica.

DAVES (see Davice, Davis), Stephen Jr. and Elizabeth Brown, Sept. 2, 1736. [Davis, C.R.]

DAVICE (see Daves, Davis), Elizabeth and James Hosmer, June 27, 1732. [Davis, and James Horsmer, C.R.]

DAVIS (see Daves, Davice), Abigail and Solomon Hartwell, Aug. 9, 1759.
Abigail and Levi Conant, June 26, 1794, in Concord.
Amos of Grafton, and Reback Colburn, Oct. 21, 1740. [Rebecca Colbourn, C.R.]

DAVIS, Anna and Abner Wheeler, June 1, 1817.
Betsey and William Stearns, Feb. 12, 1801.
Daniel and Susanna Lane, May 1, 1766.
Eleazar and Mary Davis, Sept. 3, 1756. [Eleazer, M.R.]
Eleazer and Rebecca Chandler, June 17, 1731, in Concord.
Eleazer and Rebekah Putnam, Feb. 23, 1764.
Eleazer Jr. and Martha Skinner, Jan. 1, 1799.
Eleazer P. and Emely Reed, Mar. 15, 1831.
Eleazer P. and Susan M. Sayles, Apr. 7, 1842.
Elizabeth and Ebenezer Meriam, Dec. 9, 1742.
Elizabeth and Joseph Converse, May 27, 1762, in Lexington.
Elizabeth and William Reed, Dec. 1, 1768, in Lexington.
Ephraim and Rebeckah Danforth, Mar. 21, 1737, in Billerica.
Esther and Benjamin Bacon Jr., May 27, 1766.
Eunice and Richard Wheeler, Dec. 15, 1743. C.R.
Eunice and William Marshal, Nov. 22, 1748. [Marshall, C.R. M.R.]
Hannah and John Davis Jr., Dec. 20, 1774.
Hannah and Samuel Green, Jan. 15, 1784.
Hannah and James Webber, Aug. 7, 1804.
James of New Ipswich, N.H., and Patty Bacon, Nov. 27, 1823.
Joanna and William Heartwell, Oct. 11, 1796. [Hartwell, C.R.]
John Jr. of Sliptown, and Hannah Davis, Dec. 20, 1774.
Josiah and Elizabth [Elizabeth, C.R.] Raymond, Sept. 2, 1736.
Josiah Jr. and Miriam Gilbird, Aug. 25, 1763.
Josiah and Mary Woolley, Apr. 26, 1764. [Wooley, M.R.]
Josiah and Anna Kemp, Dec. 31, 1787.
Katherine and Jacob Bacon, Feb. 13, 1768, in Lexington.
Lucy and Timothy Hartwell Jr., Oct. 7, 1790.
Lydia and Timothy Lane, Mar. 7, 1750-1.
Lydia and William Stearns, Sept. 25, 1777.
Marcy and William Raymond, Oct. 9, 1745. [Mercy, C.R.]
Mary and Timothy Hartwel, Mar. 24, 1736-7. [Hartwell, C.R.]
Mary and Ebenezer Staples, Mar. 20, 1744-5.
Mary and Eleazar [Eleazer, M.R.] Davis, Sept. 3, 1756.
Mary and Samuel Tidd, Dec. 26, 1809.
Nathanael of Rutland, and Susanna Lane, Apr. 16, 1741. C.R.
Rebeckah and Zechariah Fitch Jr., Oct. 14, 1755, in Lexington.
Rebekah and Stephen [Stephon, C.R.] Heartwell, Feb. 15, 1753. [Hartwell, M.R.]
Ruhamah and John Hill, Aug. 27, 1804.
Ruth and Samuel Lane, Oct. 2, 1760.
Salley and Joshua Page, July 15, 1802. [Sally, C.R.]
Samuel and Olive Pollard, Nov. 21, 1771.

DAVIS, Sarah and Isac [Isaac, C.R.] Meriam, Sept. 1, 1736.
Sarah and Jonathan Fassett, Oct. 27, 1761. M.R.
Sarah and Job Webber, June 21, 1796.
Simon and Allice Abbot, June 3, 1806.
Stephen Jr. and Lydia Bateman, Nov. 6, 1766.
Sukey and John Tidd, May 28, 1818.
Susan, 39, d. Eleazer and Martha, and Lewis P. Gleason, widr., Oct. 20, 1847.
Susanna and Ebenezer Richardson, Nov. 23, 1790.
Susannah and Josiah Hill, June 8, 1789, in Billerica.
Tabitha [and] Samuel Whittaker, Nov. 14, 1734, in Concord.
Thaddeus and Sarah Stearns, Sept. 28, 1779, in Billerica.
Thaddeus Jr. and Salley [Sally, C.R.] Gilson, Sept. 24, 1805.
Timothy and Hanna [Hannah, C.R.], Smith, Feb. 9, 1736-7.

DEAN, Harriett H., 27, d. Timothy and Mary, and John R. Bowen, widr., Feb. 11, 1845.
Jessee of Burlington, and Polley Bacon, Mar. 7, 1811.
Thaddeus and Sasanna Wyman, Mar. 16, 1786.
Thomas Jr. and Isabel Johnson, Apr. 24, 1770, in Woburn.

DEXTER, Samuel of Glocester, and Eliza Schaffer, Aug. 26, 1824.

DINSMORE (see Dunsmore).

DITSON, Elizabeth of Billerica, and Thomas Bacon, Apr. 11, 1749. [Elisabeth, M.R.]
Elizabeth and Abel Winship, Nov. 21, 1786.

DOLE, Cyrus of Acton, and Sarah A. Hodgman, May 26, 1836.

DRAPER, Benjamin Jr. of Boxborough, and Prisca Wyman, Nov. 14, 1816.
David of Uxbridg, and Elizabeth Simons, Feb. 21, 1733-4. [David of Uxbridge, and Elizabeth Simonds, C.R.]

DRURY, Zedekiah and Hannah Woolley, Apr. 2, 1741. C.R.

DUDLEY, Nathan of Lexington, and Hannah Lane, Jan. 20, 1804. [Jan. 20, 1805, C.R.]

DUNSMORE, Moses of Washington, and Elizabeth Reed, Feb. 13, 1794, in Acton.

DUNTON, Jemima and Nathaniel Whittemore Jr., Nov. 1, 1753. [Whittamore, C.R.]

DUREN (see Durent, Duron), Jonos of Billerica, [and] Esther Jones, Dec. 17, 1776. [Jonas, M.R.]
Polly and Stephen Parker, Jan. 30, 1791.

DURENT (see Duren, Duron), Rebecca of Billerica, and Jonas Brown Jr., Mar. 3, 1839.

DURON (see Duren, Durent), Sarah and Daniel Witney, Dec. 10, 1778.

DUTTEN (see Dutton), Samuel and Martha Lane, Aug. 19, 1740. [Dutton, C.R.]

DUTTON (see Dutten), Ann and Samuel Parkhurst, Nov. 27, 1817.
David and Hannah Whitteker, —— 13, 1760, in Lexington.
Hannah and Joshua Walton, Mar. 6, 1770, in Lexington.
Hiram L. of Andover, and Ellen Towns, Apr. 4, 1843, in Andover.
Lydia A. of Billerica, d. George and Lydia, and Joseph Foster, Nov. 8, 1849.
Patte and David Pollard, Dec. 13, 1764.
Samuel and Anna Lane, Nov. 28, 1805. [Dutten, C.R.]

EAMES, Naby of Woburn, and Asa Reed, Feb. 17, 1803. [Nabby of Woburn, and Asa Meads, C.R.]
Samuel, Dea., of Woburn, and Joanna Fasset, July 4, 1770, in Woburn.

EASTERBROOK (see Esterbrook), Lovel of Concord, and Harriet S. Nickless, Mar. 28, 1826.

EATON, Luther and Mary Crosby, Nov. 11, 1823.

EDLAND, Mary G. P., 29, d. W[illia]m and Abigail, and Lorenzo Stephens, Jan. 29, 1846.

EDWARDS, Catherine and Henry H. Staples, Dec. 8, 1836.
Rob[er]t W. of Situate, and Emeline Haynes, Oct. 10, 1841.

ELIOT, Joseph and Mary Melvin, Oct. 12, 1752. [Melven, C.R.] [Elliot, and Mary Melven, M.R.]

EMERY, Francis W. R. and Mary B. Wolcott, Mar. 26, 1839.

ESTERBROOK (see Easterbrook), Harriet S. and Isaac F. Green, Mar. 25, 1830.

EVANS, Andrew of Woburn, and Hannah Brown, Feb. 12, 1784.
Hannah and Jonas Putnam, Mar. 14, 1811.

EVERETT, William and Elizabeth Lane, Jan. 20, 1831.

FAIRBANKS, Rusa of Dedham, and Reuben Allen, June 4, 1795, in Dedham.

FARLEY, Timothy of Billerica, and Mary Richardson, Oct. 17, 1743. [Timothy Jr., C.R.]

FARMER, Abigail, Mrs., of Billerica, and Capt. James Lane, May 27, 1766, in Billerica.

FARNUM, Abner D., 22, s. Abner and Mary of Concord, N.H., and Margaret T. Crosby, Sept. 14, 1848.

FARRAR, Caroline M., 36, of Concord, d. Timothy and Matilda, and Joseph B. Hodgman, July 13 [1844].

FARREL, Sale and Richard Winship, Feb. 21, 1788.

FASSET (see Fassett), Amittai of Lexington, and John Page, Jan. 15, 1756, in Lexington.
Asa and Margaret Page, Nov. 13, 1777.
Dorothy of Lexington, and Ebenezer Page, Feb. 21, 1760. [Fassett, M.R.]
Joanna and Dea. Samuel Eames, July 4, 1770, in Woburn.
John and Mary Woolley, May 14, 1741. [Fassett, C.R.]
Joseph of Lexington, and Dorithy Pollard, May 6, 1756. [Fassett, and Dorothy Pollard, M.R.]
Josiah and Joanna Paige, Apr. 14, 1747.
Mary and Ebenezer Spawlding, Feb. 24, 1742. [Spaulding, 1742-3, C.R.]
Peter and Mary Cutor, Mar. 24, 1736-7. [Fassett, and Mary Cutter, C.R.]
Sarah and John Webber, Apr. 10, 1760. [Fassett, M.R.]
Susana and Job Lane, Jan. 29, 1746-7. [Susanna, C.R. M.R.]

FASSETT (see Fasset), Jonathan and Sarah Davis, Oct. 27, 1761. M.R.

FAY, Cyrus, Dr., of Brighton [Boulton, C.R.], and Rebecca Merriam, July 10, 1804.
Rebecca and John Jones, Nov. 28, 1816.

FELT, Moses of Lexington, and Lydia F. Clark, Apr. 29, 1816.

FISHER, Eleazer of Dunstable, N.H., and Lucy Russell, Jan. 1, 1829.

FISK (see Fiske), David of Lexington, and Cloe Trask, Aug. 10, 1820.
Elizabeth and William Whitney, Mar. 30, 1802.

FISKE (see Fisk), Betty, Mrs. [dup. Rebekah Fisk], of Lexington, and Lt. William Merriam [dup. Meriam, omits Lt.], Mar. 28, 1786, in Lexington.
George of Amherst, N.H., and Arinda Lane, May 6, 1824.

FITCH, Albert and Almira Cutler, Nov. 25 [1841].
Alford and Salley Reed, June 4, 1818.
Alice and Henry Woods Jr., May 3, 1780.
Almond and Martha Wood, Mar. 30 [1814].
Benjamin and Miriam Gray, Feb. 28, 1732, in Andover.
Betty and Noah Wyrth, Mar. 30, 1763, in Lexington.
David and Mary Fowle, Apr. 3, 1770, in Woburn.
David Jr. and Hannah Procter, Nov. 12, 1799.
David Jr. and Olive Simonds, Jan. 8, 1805, in Burlington.
Elizabeth and Samuel Lane Jr., Dec. 8, 1763. [Elisabeth, M.R.]
Elizabth and Joseph Meedes, Dec. 11, 1735. [Elizabeth, and Joseph Meeds, C.R.]
Esther and Nehemiah Lawrence, Oct. 25, 1774.
Eunice and Daniel M. Nickole, Sept. 29, 1778.
Hannah and David Tarbell, Aug. 1, 1751.
Hannah and Dr. Bela Gardner, Apr. 24, 1823.
Jeremiah and Elizabth [Elizabeth, C.R.] Lane, Feb. 3, 1735–6.
Joanna and Benjamin Tidd, Jan. 6, 1774, in Lexington.
Joel and Susanna Hill, Feb. 18, 1819.
Joseph and Sarah Grimes, Jan. 21, 1730–1.
Lois and Edward Powers, Nov. 21, 1776.
Lucy and John Page, June 5, 1810.
Lydia and Nath[anie]l Page Jr., Sept. 10, 1801.
Lydia S. and Joseph Skinner, Dec. 10, 1837.
Martha S. and Nathan O. Reed, Dec. 18, 1834.
Mary and Oliver Reed Jr., Sept. 2, 1810.
Mary F. and Benjamin F. Hartwell, Jan. 9, 1835.
Matthew and Lydia Lane, Aug. 25, 1774.
Meriam and Timothy Jaquith, Sept. 11, 1788. [Merriam, Sept. 11, 1778, M.R.]
Molley and Jonathan Blodget, Jan. 12, 1757. [Molly, M.R.]
Moses Jr. and Polley Brown, Dec. 6, 1810.
Nancy, Mrs., and Nathan O. Reed, Nov. 10, 1843.
Nathan and Louisa Burnam, Sept. 9, 1834.
Phebe and John Sprake, Apr. 1, 1784. [July 22, 1784, M.R.]
Rachel and John Page, June 3, 1773.

FITCH, Rachel and Joseph Brown, Feb. 18, 1819.
Sally and Simeon Blodgett, Oct. 25, 1804.
Sarah and Josiah Crosby, Aug. 23, 1750.
Susanna and Josiah Munroe, Nov. 16, 1768, in Lexington.
Thaddeus and Mary Moore, Sept. 14, 1779.
Zachariah of Groton, and Lydia Buck, Aug. 4, 1763, in Groton.
Zachriah and Elizabeth Grimes, Oct. 1, 1733. [Zachariah, c.r.]
Zechariah Jr. and Rebeckah Davis, Oct. 14, 1755, in Lexington.

FLAG (see Flagg), Daniel of Littleton, and Amittai Simonds, Nov. 1, 1832.

FLAGG (see Flag), Martha of Woburn, and John Lane, Oct. 28, 1747, in Woburn.
Sarah [of] Concord, [and] Nathan Woolley, Oct. 3, 1754, in Concord.

FLETCHER, Samuel of Westford, and Lydia Webber, Apr. 18, 1805. [Samuel Jr., c.r.]

FLINT, Betsey Winchester of Dracutt, and Edward Sheaf Brown, Sept. 11, 1799, in Dracutt.
Edward and Sarah Bacon, Apr. 21, 1831.

FORBUSH, Lois of Acton, and James Simons, July 9, 1789, in Acton.
Loiza E., 22, of Carlisle, d. Paul and Hannah, and Samuel E. Scott, May 12, 1844.

FOSTER, Joseph of Billerica, s. Samuel and Anna of Billerica, and Lydia A. Dutton, Nov. 8, 1849.
Noah and Grace Lane, Mar. 19, 1799.

FOTHINGHAM, William of Billerica, and Abigail Thompson, Oct. 20, 1805.

FOWLE, Mary of Woburn, and David Fitch, Apr. 3, 1770, in Woburn.

FRANCES (see Francis), Sullivan R., widr., of Weathersfield, Ill., and Mary S. Gardner, July 12, 1846.

FRANCIS (see Frances), John and Jane Teal, June 3, 1777. [Teel, m.r.]

FRAZER, George of Boston, and Elizabeth B. Webber, Nov. 19, 1826.

FREEMAN, Pompey and Lois Hill, June 20, 1773, in Bridgwater.
Rebecca of Westfield, and Daniel Cooley, Aug. 8, 1745, in Westfield.

FRENCH, Abigail of Andover, and Rev. Samuel Stearns, May 9, 1797, in Andover.
Esther, of Billerica, and Nathan [Nathaniel, M.R.] Bowman, May 30, 1771.
Hannah of Billerica, and Samuel Lane, Jan. 6, 1774, in Billerica.
Jonas of Billerica, and Hannah Page, Jan. 5, 1758.
Susanna and William Goodrige, Jan. 8, 1824.

FRINK, Electa and George W. Hewes, Feb. 8, 1844.

FROST, William F. and Rebecca Cutler, Mar. 15, 1842.

FROTHINGHAM (see Fothingham).

FRYE, Hannah of Andover, and John Bowman, Sept. 19, 1781, in Andover.

FULLER, Augustus R. of Dunstable, N.H., and Hannah Elizabeth Brown, Sept. 23, 1833.
Elisha of Middleton [Middlaton, C.R.], and Elizabeth [Elisabeth, C.R. M.R.] Putnam, Nov. 28, 1752.
Emeline and George A. Gillet, Oct. —, 1831.
Henry H. and Elmira Wilson, Aug. 4, 1834.
Lucy of Newton, and Joseph Mead, Apr. 16, 1767, in Newton.
Mary W. and John P. Buttrick, June —, 1827.

GARDNER, Bela, Dr., and Hannah Fitch, Apr. 24, 1823.
Edward and Elizabeth Preese, Feb. 29, 1776. [Elisabeth Preose, Feb. 19, M.R.]
Mary S. of Lowell, d. Bela and Hannah, and Sullivan R. Frances, widr., July 12, 1846.

GIBSON, James of Lowell, and Mary L. Wright, Apr. 17, 1831.
Jane D. and John Simonds, July 31, 1828.

GILBIRD, Miriam and Josiah Davis Jr., Aug. 25, 1763.

GILLET, George A. of Hebron, Conn., and Emeline Fuller, Oct. —, 1831.

GILMAN, Nathan D. and Attella Meigs, Apr. 28, 1839.

GILSON, Salley and Thaddeus Davis Jr., Sept. 24, 1805. [Sally, C.R.]
Samuel of Pepperil, and Sarah Lane, Nov. 26, 1778.

GLEASON, Benj[amin] of Andover, and Rhoda Gleason, May 22, 1803. [May 26, c.r.]

Caroline and Daniel Clark, Apr. 14, 1834.
Dolley and James Willson Jr., Mar. 8, 1798. [Dolly, and James Wilson Jr., c.r.]
Elizabeth and David Clark, Oct. 21, 1834.
Hannah and Caleb Harrington White, June 28, 1799. [June 20, c.r.]
Jonas and Abigail Danforth, Jan. 20, 1795, in Billerica.
Josiah B., 29, of Billerica, s. William and Sarah, and Mary Hartwell, Nov. 27, 1845.
Lewis P. and Sophronia Butler, Mar. 3, 1826.
Lewis P. and Lucy Butler, Oct. 2, 1827.
Lewis P., widr., 47, s. John and Elizabeth, and Susan Davis, Oct. 20, 1847.
Mary W. and William Webber, Oct. 11, 1835.
Rhoda and Benj[amin] Gleason, May 22, 1803. [May 26, c.r.]
Simeon and Susanna Parker Jones, May 29, 1804.
William Jr. of Billerica, and Sally Bacon, Feb. 11, 1795, in Billerica.

GOLDSMITH, Jeremiah of Andover, and Sarah Convass, Dec. 30, 178[ ] [? 1788]. [Convers, Dec. 30, 1778, m.r.]

GOODELL, Amos and Eame [? Ame] Rea, June 3, 176[ ]. [Anne, June 3, 1762, m.r.]

GOODRICH (see Goodridge, Goodrige), William [of] Weathersfield, Vt., [and] Hannah Bowman, July 2, 1791, in Concord.

GOODRIDGE (see Goodrich, Coodrige), Charlotte and Sardis Johnson, Mar. 16, 1826.
Francis B. and Mary Cutler, Feb. 9, 1832.

GOODRIGE (see Goodrich, Goodridge), Sophia and Abel Shed, Dec. 9, 1819.
William and Susanna French, Jan. 8, 1824.

GOODWIN, Henry and Sarah Lane, Sept. 20, 1838.
Joseph, widr., 25, s. Uriah and Nancy, and Catherine A. Lane, Oct. 5, 1845.
Thomas, widr., 46, of Littleton, s. Uriah and Mary, and Eliza Longley, Feb. 9 [1845].
William and Eliza J. Cutler, May 26, 1836.

GOULD, Pamelia and Benjamin Hosmer, June 9, 1816.

GOULD, Simion of Stoddard, and Rhoda Lane, Feb. 12, 1789. [Simon, M.R.]

GOWING, Micajah of Wilmington, and Clarissa Hosmer, Jan. 2, 1814.

GRAGG, Amelia and Josiah Stearns Lane, Feb. 11, 1813.
Caroline and Isaac Blanchard, Oct. 27, 1840.
Charles of Boston, and Eliot Reed, Nov. 15, 1821.
Helen M., d. Charles O. and Eliot, and Amos W. Hill, Apr. 3, 1849, in Providence, R.I.
Louisa and Justus P. Hastings, Apr. 14, 1840.
Lucy, 20, d. Charles and Elliott, and Zebediah Hollis, May 2, 1844.
William, Rev., of Carlisle, and Mary Pollard, Jan. 29, 1833.
William A. and Rebecca Willard, Mar. 1, 1840.

GRAY, Miriam of Andover, and Benjamin Fitch, Feb. 28, 1732, in Andover.
Robert and Ann Mallow, Mar. 11, 1762, in Methuen.

GREEN, Isaac F. of Townsend, and Harriet S. Esterbrook, Mar. 25, 1830.
Isaiah of Carlisle, and Hannah Lane, Dec. 13, 1801. [Isaah, C.R.]
Samuel of Lincoln, and Hannah Davis, Jan. 15, 1784.

GRIFFIN, Elizabeth and William Johnson Lawrence, Nov. 26, 1797.

GRIMES, Elizabeth and Zachriah [Zachariah, C.R.] Fitch, Oct. 1, 1733.
Jonathan and Jane Hutchinson, Feb. 18, 1745–6.
Mary and Nathaniel [Nathanael, C.R.] Paige Sr., June 23, 1748. [Page, M.R.]
Ruth and Will[ia]m Hasttens, Dec. 2, 1740. [Hastings, C.R.]
Sarah and Joseph Fitch, Jan. 21, 1730–1.
William and Mary Whetnee, Jan. 1, 1740–1. [Whitney, C.R.]

GROSVENOR (see Grovner).

GROVES, Ezra of Groton, and Sarah Reed, Sept. 14 [1813].

GROVNER, ——— of Lexington, and Sally Merriam, Dec. 28, 1812.

HADLEY, Alice of Lexington, and Samuel Merriam, Feb. 21, 1785, in Lexington.

HADLEY, Israel Porter of Cambridge, and Sally Porter, July 14, 1816.
Lydia and Josiah H. Willis, Nov. 28, 1822.
Mary and Job Lane, Aug. 16, 1815.
Simon of Lexington, and Olive Porter, Jan. 27, 1791. [Jan. 30, M.R.]
Thomas Jr. of Lexington, and Alice Newton, Sept. 16, 1773.

HAGGET, Amos of Concord, and Susanna Page, Jan. 16, 1781.
Sarah [dup. Haggit] and Jonathan Pollard, May 11, 1762.

HALL, Elizabeth and James Simonds, June 30, 1763, in Lexington.
Hannah and Benjamin Stevens, Oct. 25, 1782.

HARRINGTON (see Herington), Abigail and David Constantine, Aug. 5, 1838, in Burlington.
Sukey and Levi Willson, Apr. 8, 1813.
Thomas of Lexington, and Lucy Perry, July 4, 1771, in Lexington.

HARTWEL (see Hartwell, Heartwel, Heartwell), Danel [and] Mrs. Sarah Wilson, June 13, 1734. [Daniel Hartwell and Sarah Willsson, C.R.]
Timothy and Mary Davis, Mar. 24, 1736–7. [Hartwell, C.R.]

HARTWELL (see Hartwel, Heartwel, Heartwell), Benjamin F. and Mary F. Fitch, Jan. 9, 1835.
Dolley and Abraham Whitcomb, May 27, 1804.
Eldridge, s. W[illia]m and w., and Lucy P. Reed, Nov. 1, 1843.
Elizabeth and Robert Reed, Mar. 2, 1771, in Lexington.
Hannah and John Skilton, June 4, 1805.
Jemime and Ebenezer Cummings, June 22, 1774. [Jemima, and Ebenezer Cumings, M.R.]
John and Mrs. Mary Hill, Dec. 3, 1744, in Billerica.
John and Elizabeth Moore, Apr. 17, 1787. [Moor, M.R.]
Joseph and Jemima Bachelder, Dec. 12, 1750, in Beverly.
Joseph and Elizabeth Mead, July 3, 1804. [Meads, C.R.]
Louisa and Elias Skelton, Dec. 2, 1830.
Mary [and] John Page, Dec. 31, 1730, in Concord.
Mary, 20, d. Amos and Louisa, and Josiah B. Gleason, Nov. 27, 1845.
Molley and Poulter Reed, Sept. 1, 1789. [Molly, M.R.]
Ruth and Daze Skelton, June 19, 1770, in Woburn.
Ruth and Joseph Porter Jr., June 3, 1788.
Samuel and Desire Brown, Oct. 26, 1779.

HARTWELL, Solomon and Abigail Davis, Aug. 9, 1759.
Stephen and Sarah Reed, Jan. 19, 1775, in Lexington.
Timothy Jr. and Lucy Davis, Oct. 7, 1790.
William and Mary Lake, Apr. 6, 1809.

HASTINGS (see Hasttens), Justus P. and Louisa Gragg, Apr. 14, 1840.
Samuel of Waltham, and Susanna Lane, Nov. 28, 1805.

HASTTENS (see Hastings), Will[ia]m and Ruth Grimes, Dec. 2, 1740. [Hastings, C.R.]

HATCH, Almira of Lowell, and Phinehas W. Chamberlain, May 12, 1831.
Charlotte and Edward Bacon, Nov. 28, 1839.
Lydia P. and David Hill, Dec. 27, 1832.

HAYDEN, Almira, 20, of Wesford, d. Luther and Betsey, and William S. Comey, Apr. 13, 1845.
Nathaniel of Sudbury, and Abigail Temple, Sept. 29, 1731, in Sudbury.

HAYNES, Emeline and Rob[er]t W. Edwards, Oct. 10, 1841.
Rachel and Henry Johnson, July 6, 1834.
Stephens Jr., 29, s. Stephen and Rachel, and Catherine D. Butler, Sept. 5, 1847.

HAYWARD (see Howard), Ebenezer and Sarah Lane, May 15, 1817.
Ebenezer and Esther Buttrick, Nov. 27, 1828.
Ebenezer of Carlisle, and Mrs. Mary Pierce, Mar. 27, 1832.
James of Acton, and Polley Lawrence, [July] 23, 1818.
John W. and Lydia W. Lane, Apr. 26, 1827.
Mather of Boxborough, and Lucy Page, May 1, 1800.
Moses and Lucretia Bingham, Apr. 30, 1829.

HAZELETT, Caroline and Thomas Crawford, Jan. 1, 1839.

HEALD, Hannah, 24, b. Carlisle, of Carlisle, d. Cyrus and Charlotte of Carlisle, and Thomas B. Hosmer, July 29, 1849.

HEARTWEL (see Hartwel, Hartwell, Heartwell), Stephen and Mary Raymond, Dec. 31, 1741. [Heartwell, C.R.]

HEARTWELL (see Hartwel, Hartwell, Heartwel), Abigail and John Simonds, Jan. 9, 1766.
Mary and Francis Willson Jr., May 11, 1762. [Hartwell, M.R.]

HEARTWELL, Stephen and Rebekah Davis, Feb. 15, 1753.
[Stephon, C.R.] [Hartwell, M.R.]
William and Joanna Davis, Oct. 11, 1796. [Hartwell, C.R.]

HEATH, Alvina and Francis Wilson Jr., Feb. 7, 1828.

HERINGTON (see Harrington), Abigel and Daniel Rolfe, June 11, 1746. [Abigail Harrington, C.R. M.R.]

HEWES, George W. of Boston, and Electa Frink, Feb. 8, 1844.

HILDRETH, Sarah, wid., of Andover, and John Lane Jr., May 28, 1761, in Andover.

HILL, Amos W., b. Cambridge, of Cambridge, s. —— of Cambridge, and Helen M. Gragg, Apr. 3, 1849, in Providence, R.I.
Anna of Billerica, and Lt. Abner Stearns, May 1, 1796.
Constantine and Martha Pratt, Nov. 7, 1835.
David and Lydia P. Hatch, Dec. 27, 1832.
Ebenezer, Rev. of Mason, and Nabby Stearns, Sept. 22, 1799.
Hannah of Billerica, and Oliver Pollard, Feb. 17, 1735-6, in Billerica.
John and Duhamah [Ruhamah, C.R.] Davis, Aug. 27, 1804.
Jonathan of Billerica, and Mary Lane, Jan. 13, 1746-7 [dup. in Billerica]. [Jonathan Jr., C.R. M.R.]
Jonathan of Billerica, and Mary Proctor, Dec. 13, 1798, in Billerica.
Josiah of Billerica, and Susannah Davis, June 8, 1789, in Billerica.
Lois of Bridgwater, and Pompey Freeman, June 20, 1773, in Bridgwater.
Mary, Mrs., of Billerica, and John Hartwell, Dec. 3, 1744, in Billerica.
Mary and Moses Abbott, Apr. 15, 1755, in Charlestown.
Mary of Billerica, and Oliver Pollard, June 19, 1777, in Billerica.
Patte of Billerica, and William Page, Dec. 8, 1763, in Billerica.
Sally [dup. Salley] [and] Joseph Merriam, Feb. 27, 1794, in Concord.
Susanna and Joel Fitch, Feb. 18, 1819.

HOAR, Edward and Betsey Wright, Nov. 29, 1827.

HODGMAN, Elizabeth, Mrs., and Dea. Phinehas Wheeler, Sept. 15, 1831.
Elizabeth and John Butterfield, Sept. 24, 1840.
Hannah of Ashby, and James Clark, May 28, 1818.

HODGMAN, Harriat and Samuel Reed, May 12, 1825.
John and Lucy Wheeler, Aug. 22, 1832.
Joseph B. and Mary Adeline Merriam, Mar. 7, 1833.
Joseph B., widr., 40, s. John and Elizabeth, and Caroline M. Farrar, July 13 [1844].
Sarah A. and Cyrus Dole, May 26, 1836.

HOLLIS, Zebediah, 28, b. Littleton, s. Zebediah and Eunice, and Lucy Gragg, May 2, 1844.

HOSMER, Ann and William Brockway, Dec. 1, 1808.
Benjamin and Pamelia Gould, June 9, 1816.
Castalio and Ruth Pool, Dec. 19, 1805. [Castatio, C.R.]
Clarissa and Micajah Gowing, Jan. 2, 1814.
Gustavus and Julia Wilson, Apr. 2, 1822.
Henry and Catherine G. Cook, Apr. 6, 1843.
James of Concord, and Elizabeth Davice, June 27, 1732. [Horsmer, and Elizabeth Davis, C.R.]
Joseph and Martha Bacon, Oct. 1, 1837.
Laura, 28, d. Castalio and Ruth, and Leander Clark, June 29, 1845.
Leander and Sophronia Wilson, Mar. 5, 1818.
Malvina, 19, d. Gustavus and Julia, and Charles E. Manning, Apr. 23, 1846.
Maria, d. Leander and w., and Nathaniel P. Watts, Oct. 12, 1843.
Martha and Thompson Bacon, Oct. 16, 1783.
Martha and Benjamin Clark, May 6, 1812.
Martha E., 20, d. Leander and w., and Isaac L. Watts, June 17, 1847.
Thomas B., 26, s. Leander and Sophronia, and Hannah Heald, July 29, 1849.

HOVEY, Elizabeth, 34, d. Caleb and Ann, and Jacob Wheeler, Nov. 24 [1844].

HOWARD (see Hayward), Abigal and John Meriam, Mar. 23, 1730-1. [Abigail, C.R.]
William of Acton, and Jemima Whitmore, Mar. 9, 1782. [Hayward, M.R.]

HUBBARD, Benjamin of Rindge, N.H., and Dorcas White, Apr. 3, 1811.
Hezekiah of Ringe, and Rebecca Hutchinson, May 30, 1781.

HULL, Stephen and Harriot Rice, Nov. 18 [1841].

HUNT, Rebecca of Lowell, and Larkin P. Page, Dec. 3, 1829.
Sarah of Concord, and William Convers, Nov. 13, 1800.

HURD, Isaac W. of Concord, and Caroline Bacon, May 14, 1837.

HUTCHINSON, Benjamin Jr. and Rebekah Lane, July 31, 1750.
Bette and Samuel Parkhust, Feb. 12, 1788. [Betty Hutchenson and Samuel Parkhurst, M.R.]
Elizabeth and Samuel Stearns, Oct. 31, 1749. [Elisabeth, M.R.]
Jane and Jonathan Grimes, Feb. 18, 1745-6.
Molly and Samuel Paige, Nov. 23, 1775. [Page, M.R.]
Nathan and Rachel Stearns, Apr. 16, 1741, in Billerica.
Rebecca and Hezekiah Hubbard, May 30, 1781.
Sarah and Israel Putnam Jr., Jan. 3, 1748-9.
Sarah and Zebediah Rogers, May 4, 1790.

INGLES, James and Margaret Benner, Mar. 13, 1788 [?], in Billerica.

IRELAND, Josiah of Charlestown, and Anna Brown, Aug. 22, 1770, in Lexington.

JACKSON, Hannah, Mrs., of Plymouth, and Rev. Joseph Penniman, Oct. 10, 1771, in Plymouth.
Joshua, 24, s. Josiah and Deborah, and Mary Pierce, Nov. 28 [1844].
Lucy of Plymouth, and Dr. Stephen Miner, Oct. 30, 1783, in Plymouth.

JACOBS, John of Middleton, and Mary Putnam, June 19, 1760.

JAMES, Charles, Dea., of Medford, and Elizabeth W. Stearns, Dec. 8, 1831.

JAQUITH, Timothy and Abigail Lewis, May 29, 1788. [May 28, M.R.]
Timothy of Billerica, and Meriam Fitch, Sept. 11, 1788. [Merriam, Sept. 11, 1778, M.R.]

JEFFERDS, Forest, Rev., of Epping, N.H., and Sarah Caroline Stearns, Sept. 27, 1827.

JEWETT, Walter E., 31, of Pepperell, s. Edmund J. and Phebe of Pepperell, and Susan Peirce, Dec. 19, 1848.

JOHNSON, Henry and Rachel Haynes, July 6, 1834.
Isabel and Thomas Dean Jr., Apr. 24, 1770, in Woburn.

JOHNSON, Obadiah P. and Abigail M. Reed, Jan. 3, 1833.
Rachel, 30, d. Steven Haines and Rachel, and William H. Cooper, widr., Dec. 27, 1846.
Sardis and Charlotte Goodridge, Mar. 16, 1826.

JONES, Abigail [of] Concord, [and] Daniel Page, Oct. 10, 1765, in Concord.
Esther [and] Jonos [Jonas, M.R.] Duren, Dec. 17, 1776.
James Carey and Mary Coad, July 19, 1787.
John and Rebecca Fay, Nov. 28, 1816.
Lucy and Samuel Lane 3d, May 28, 1801.
Mary [of] Concord, [and] Jonathan Taylor, Aug. 29, 1754, in Concord.
Nabby and Lt. Edward Stearns, Jan. 1, 1798.
Polly [and] Edward [dup. Edwerd] Stearns, Dec. 23, 1794, in Concord.
Rebekah and Samuel Ball, Nov. 4, 1784.
Ruth [of] Concord, [and] David Taylor, Feb. 5, 1745, in Concord.
Susanna Parker and Simeon Gleason, May 29, 1804.
Timothy [and] Rebecca Putnam, Nov. 1, 1768, in Concord.
Timothy and Susanna Wilkens, June 17, 1806. [Willson, C.R.]

KEMP, Anna and Josiah Davis, Dec. 31, 1787.

KENDAL (see Kendall), Alace and David Whittomore, Mar. 11, 1730–1. [Allice, and David Whittermore, C.R.]

KENDALL (see Kendal), Dorcas and Wyman Skelton, May 13, 1819.

KENT, Isaac and Mary Mansfield, May 4, 1749.

KIDDER, Benjamin and Hannah Richardson, Nov. 9, 1731, in Billerica.

KINSMAN, Timothy of Lincoln, "Late of N.H.," and Lucy S. Abbott, Mar. 16, 1809.

LADD, John S., widr., 37, of Cambridge, and Mary Ann Butler, Sept. 5, 1847.

LAKE, Mary and William Hartwell, Apr. 6, 1809.

LANE, Abigail R., 21, d. O. W. and Catherine, and Samuel S. Wilson, Oct. 16, 1847.
Amittai and Elijah Bacon, ———, 1785. [Amity, Dec. 15, M.R.]
Anna and Samuel Dutton, Nov. 28, 1805. [Dutten, C.R.]

LANE, Arinda and George Fiske, May 6, 1824.
Benjamin and Anna Page, Dec. 9, 1779.
Bethiah and John Webber Jr., Dec. 15, 1785. [Bethia, M.R.]
Catherine and Silas Wilkins, Apr. 29, 1830.
Catherine A., 21, d. Oliver W. and Catherine, and Joseph Goodwin, widr., Oct. 5, 1845.
David and Molley Lane, Oct. 11, 1781.
David and Phebe Lane, Apr. 30, 1822.
Dorcas and Nathan Whit, Jan. 3, 1788.
Eliab Banidge and Anna Wellington, Mar. 21, 1802. [Willington, C.R.]
Elizabeth and Matthew Pollard, May 8, 1800.
Elizabeth and William Everett, Jan. 20, 1831.
Elizabth and Jeremiah Fitch, Feb. 3, 1735-6. [Elizabeth, C.R.]
Elizebeth [Elizabeth, C.R.] and Michael Bacon, Mar. 5, 1746-7. [Elisabeth, M.R.]
Elliot Reed and Asa Webber, Apr. 30, 1801. [Eliot Reed, C.R.]
Esther and Joseph Crosby, Sept. 24, 1778.
Grace and Noah Foster, Mar. 19, 1799.
Hannah and John Bacon, May 6, 1779.
Hannah and Jonathan Lane, Feb. 1, 1787.
Hannah and Isaiah [Isaah, C.R.] Green, Dec. 13, 1801.
Hannah and Nathan Dudley, Jan. 20, 1804. [Jan. 20, 1805, C.R.]
Hannah and Elijah Putnam, Sept. 27, 1838.
Hannah A. and Charles C. Corey, Nov. 27, 1839.
James Jr. and Mary Wellington, Jan. 10, 1750-1.
James, Capt., and Cherry Wellington, Aug. 9, 1763, in Lexington.
James, Capt., and Mrs. Abigail Farmer, May 27, 1766, in Billerica.
James, Capt., and Mrs. Abigail Meriam, Jan. 20, 1774.
James and Molley Pollard, June 6, 1805.
Job and Susana Fasset, Jan. 29, 1746-7. [Susanna, C.R. M.R.]
Job and Mrs. Elizabeth Stickney, Jan. 15, 1777.
Job and Mary Hadley, Aug. 16, 1815.
John and Hannah Abbott, Mar. 16, 1732, in Andover.
John Jr. and Ruth Bowman, Feb. 13, 1745-6.
John and Martha Flagg, Oct. 28, 1747, in Woburn.
John Jr. and Sarah Hildreth, wid., May 28, 1761, in Andover.
John " Tertiary " [*tertius*] and Ruhamah Reed, Nov. 25, 1773, in Lexington.
Jonathan and Hannah Lane, Feb. 1, 1787.
Jonathan and Ruhamah Page, July 27, 1815.
Josiah Stearns and Amelia Gragg, Feb. 11, 1813.
Katharine and Benjamin Bacon, Feb. 15, 1738-9.

BEDFORD MARRIAGES. 87

LANE, Lois, d. Amasa and Cyrus F. Crosby, Jan. 9, 1844.
Lucy and Elijah Stearns, Dec. 20, 1759. [Feb. 20, 1760, M.R.]
Lucy and Jonathan Putnam, Nov. 23, 1775.
Luke and Hannah Crosby, Mar. 24, 1791, in Billerica.
Lydia and Matthew Fitch, Aug. 25, 1774.
Lydia W. and John W. Hayward, Apr. 26, 1827.
Martha and John Whitmore, Dec. 30, 1736.
Martha and Samuel Dutten, Aug. 19, 1740. [Dutton, C.R.]
Martha and Joshua Bond, June 12, 1775. [Jan. 12, M.R.]
Mary and Jonathan Hill [Jr., C.R. M.R.], Jan. 13, 1746-7 [dup. in Billerica].
Mary and John Moore, Nov. 21, 1799, in Billerica.
Mary Elizabeth and Jephthah Parkhurst, Apr. 13, 1837.
Mary M., 20, d. Roger and Zelina, and Hiram Clark, Feb. 4, 1847.
Mary P. and Amos B. Cutler, Apr. 16, 1833.
Mary W. and George Briggs, Sept. 26, 1841.
Molley and David Lane, Oct. 11, 1781.
Molly and Thad[deu]s Willson, Mar. 11, 1802. [Wilson, C.R.]
Oliver A. and Catherine Walton, [July] 23, 1818.
Oliver W. and Mrs. Harriet Blinn, Feb. 26, 1843.
Phebe and David Lane, Apr. 30, 1822.
Polley and John Stearns, Feb. 10, 1801. [Polly, C.R.]
Rebekah and Benjamin Hutchinson Jr., July 31, 1750.
Rhoda and Simion [Simon, M.R.] Gould, Feb. 12, 1789.
Ruhamah and Dr. Amariah Preston, May 15, 1796.
Ruth and John Whiting, Dec. 29, 1772.
Ruth and Nathaniel Brown, Mar. 30, 1797.
Samuel and Ruth Davis, Oct. 2, 1760.
Samuel Jr. and Elizabeth [Elisabeth, M.R.] Fitch, Dec. 8, 1763.
Samuel and Hannah French, Jan. 6, 1774, in Billerica.
Samuel and Mrs. Frances Blood, May 21, 1799, in Carlisle.
Samuel 3d and Lucy Jones, May 28, 1801.
Sarah and James Miller, Dec. 28, 1732.
Sarah and Samuel Gilson, Nov. 26, 1778.
Sarah and Timothy Stearns, Nov. 1, 1787.
Sarah, wid., and Benjamin Parker, July 14, 1791.
Sarah and Ebenezer Hayward, May 15, 1817.
Sarah and Henry Goodwin, Sept. 20, 1838.
Solomon and Sarah Stearns, May 29, 1781.
Stephen and Allice Abbott, May 1, 1806. [Abbot, C.R.]
Susan G. and Nathaniel C. Cutler, Mar. 10, 1831.
Susanna and Nathanael Davis, Apr. 16, 1741. C.R.
Susanna and Daniel Davis, May 1, 1766.

LANE, Susanna and Samuel Hastings, Nov. 28, 1805.
Sylvania and Benjamin Bacon 3d, Apr. 7, 1822.
Timothy and Lydia Davis, Mar. 7, 1750–1.
Ziba and Lydia Danforth, Apr. 1, 1778, in Billerica.

LAWHEAD, Ann Jane, b. Ireland, d. —— of Ireland, and Samuel Taylor, widr., Feb. 8, 1843.

LAWRENCE, Bezaliel and Abigail Simonds, Feb. 12, 1786, in Leominster.
Jonathan of Lexington, and Polly Reed, Apr. 12, 1798, in Lexington.
Lavinia and Lucius Stiles, Sept. 11, 1843.
Lucy Ann and Warren Bacon, Aug. 1, 1841.
Nehemiah of Groton, and Esther Fitch, Oct. 25, 1774.
Polley and James Hayward, [July] 23, 1818.
Sylvanus and Hannah Malvina Swain Reed, Nov. 6, 1839.
William Johnson of Littleton, and Elizabeth Griffin, Nov. 26, 1797.

LEWIS, Abigail of Billerica, and Timothy Jaquith, May 29, 1788. [May 28, M.R.]

LIBBE, Lucy F. and William Porter, May 4, 1779.

LITCHFIELD, Francis of Cohasset, and Sophia Patten, Oct. 10, 1841.
Joseph, 30, s. William, and Theresa E. Webber, Sept. 18, 1845.

LOCK, Job of Lexington, and Phillis Mannuel, Jan. 14, 1790. [Manuel, Jan. 14, 1789, M.R.]

LONGLEY, Eliza, 43, d. Asa and Betsey, and Thomas Goodwin, widr., Feb. 9 [1845].

LORING, Joseph Jr. of Lexington, and Betty Pollard, Nov. 26, 1772, in Lexington.

LUN, Lucy Gardner and James Pont, Feb. 28, 1793, in Lunenburg.

MALLOW, Ann of Methuen, and Robert Gray, Mar. 11, 1762, in Methuen.

MANN, Alexander of Charlestown, and Dorcas Rice, Mar. 25, 1838.

MANNING, Charles E., 24, s. Peter and Nancy, and Malvina Hosmer, Apr. 23, 1846.
Lydia Ann and Seth Whitford, Feb. 19, 1835.

MANNUEL, Phillis and Job Lock, Jan. 14, 1790. [Manuel, Jan. 14, 1789, M.R.]

MANSFIELD, Joel, 22, b. Chelmsford, s. Joel and Rebecca of Chelmsford, and Maria L. Bacon, Mar. 4, 1847.
Mary and Isaac Kent, May 4, 1749.

MARSHAL (see Marshall), William of Concord, and Eunice Davis, Nov. 22, 1748. [Marshall, C.R. M.R.]

MARSHALL (see Marshal), James Jr. of Chelmsford, and Sarah Skinner, Apr. 9, 1816.
Molley and Abel Butters, May 24, 1812.

MASON, Sarah of Concord, and John Bannon, Sept. 25, 1843.

MAXWEL (see Maxwell), William and Sarah Bowman, Nov. 23, 1773. [Maxwell, Nov. 23, 1775, M.R.]

MAXWELL (see Maxwel), Benjamin and Annar [Anna, M.R.] Winslow, Jan. 7, 1762.
Francis B. and Susanna Preston, Mar. 19, 1812.
Hugh and Bridgett Munroe, Nov. 4, 1760, in Lexington.
Margaret and Andrew Thompson, June 30, 1756.

MAY, Betsey and Joshua Page, Nov. 20, 1728.

McAULEY, Nancy, Mrs., and Michael Burk, Dec. 3, 1839.

McILLVANE, Eleanor and Samuel Boyd, Nov. 21, 1745. [Nov. 18, C.R.]

MEAD (see Meedes, Meeds), Elizabeth and Joseph Hartwell, July 3, 1804. [Meads, C.R.]
Hannah of Lexington, and James Tisdale, Aug. 13, 1772. M.R.
Joseph and Lucy Fuller, Apr. 16, 1767, in Newton.
Lydia A. and Samuel Richardson, May 29, 1832.

MEEDES (see Mead, Meeds), Joseph and Elizabth Fitch, Dec. 11, 1735. [Meeds, and Elizabeth Fitch, C.R.]

MEEDS (see Mead, Meedes), Lydia and Abijah Thompson, July 1, 1790.
Stephen and Desire Brown, Feb. 5, 1765. [Mead, M.R.]

MEIGS, Attella and Nathan D. Gilman, Apr. 28, 1839.

MELVIN, Hannah [of] Concord, [and] Jonathan Putnam, Aug. 21, 1750, in Concord.

MELVIN, Mary and Joseph Eliot, Oct. 12, 1752. [Melven, C.R.] [Melven, and Joseph Elliot, M.R.]

MERIAM (see Merriam), Abigail, Mrs., and Capt. James Lane, Jan. 20, 1774.
Abraham and Hannah Bowman, Apr. 6, 1778.
Ebenezer of Concord, and Elizabeth Davis, Dec. 9, 1742.
Isac and Sarah Davis, Sept. 1, 1736. [Isaac, C.R.]
John and Abigal [Abigail, C.R.] Howard, Mar. 23, 1730–1.
John Jr. and Hannah Brooks, Dec. 4, 1760.
Lydia, Mrs., and Rev. Nathaniel Sherman, Mar. 1, 1759. [Shearman, M.R.]
Nathaniel and Olive Wheeler, Dec. 27, 1748. [Nathanael, C.R.]
Rebekah and Joseph Stone, Jan. 13, 1758.
Sarah and David Wheeler, Dec. 27, 1733. C.R.

MERIL, Nathan and Susanna Bacon, Jan. 21, 1788. [Morril, M.R.]

MERRIAM (see Meriam), Anna and Thomas Page, Jan. 1, 1756, in Lexington.
Esther [dup. Meriam] and John Page, Feb. 14, 1792. [Meriam, M.R.]
Hannah [dup. Meriam] and John Reed Jr., Dec. 1, 1785. [Meriam, M.R.]
John [dup. Meriam] and Mary Reed, Dec. 3, 1799, in Lexington.
John A. and Nancy Bacon, Apr. 14, 1830.
Joseph of Mason, N.H., and Salley [dup. Sally] Hill, Feb. 27, 1794 [dup. in Concord].
Mary and Ephraim Crosby, Apr. 17, 1755, in Billerica.
Mary Adeline and Joseph B. Hodgman, Mar. 7, 1833.
Rebecca and Dr. Cyrus Fay, July 10, 1804.
Sally and ——— Grovner, Dec. 28, 1812.
Samuel and Alice Hadley, Feb. 21, 1785, in Lexington.
Sarah and Zebulon Convasse, May 8, 1773. [Meriam, and Zebulon Converse, M.R.]
Susan and Dr. Abel B. Adams, Apr. 25, 1841.
William and Esther Bellamy, Nov. 30, 1769.
William, Lt. [dup. Meriam, omits Lt.], and Mrs. Betty Fiske [dup. Rebekah Fisk], Mar. 28, 1786, in Lexington.

MERRILL (see Meril).

MILLER, Belinda and Nicholas M. Bean, Oct. 13, 1842.
James of Charlestown [Charlstown, C.R.], and Sarah Lane, Dec. 28, 1732.
Mary and James C. Russell, Dec. 12, 1826.

MINER, Stephen, Dr., and Lucy Jackson, Oct. 30, 1783, in Plymouth.

MONROE (see Munroe), Abel S. and Sarah Wright, Apr. 26, 1838.
Abel S., widr., 37, s. Asa and Lois, and Caroline Bacon, Nov. 28 [1844].
Jonas and Abigail F. Stearns, Nov. 24, 1831.

MOOR (see Moore), Lydia and Bradley Bowers, Feb. 19, 1793.

MOORE (see Moor), Elizabeth and John Hartwell, Apr. 17, 1787. [Moor, M.R.]
John and Elizabeth Whellor, Sept. 4, 1740. [Moor, and Elizabeth Wheeler, C.R.]
John Jr. and Mary Wheeler, July 17, 1759. [Moor, M.R.]
John and Mary Lane, Nov. 21, 1799, in Billerica.
Joseph and Dorcas [Dorothy, M.R.] Wood, Feb. 22, 1753.
Mary and Thaddeus Fitch, Sept. 14, 1779.

MORRIL (see Meril).

MULLIKIN, Mary of Concord, and Asa Porter, June 17, 1817.

MUNROE (see Monroe), Bridgett and Hugh Maxwell, Nov. 4, 1760, in Lexington.
Clariot P., 17, d. Jona[than] and Elmira, and James S. Atcherson, July 26, 1848.
Josiah of Lexington, and Susanna Fitch, Nov. 16, 1768, in Lexington.

NEWHALL, Joseph S. Jr. of Sangor [?], and Emeline A. Ware, May 25, 1841.

NEWTON, Alice and Thomas Hadley Jr., Sept. 16, 1773.

NICKLESS (see Nickole, Nicloss), Harriet S. and Lovel Easterbrook, Mar. 28, 1826.

NICKOLE (see Nickless, Niclass), Daniel M. of Rutland, and Eunice Fitch, Sept. 29, 1778.

NICLASS (see Nickless, Nickole), Stephen R. of Westford, and Sally M. Stearns, Oct. 22, 1829.

NUTTING, John and Hannah Reed, July 10, 1754, in Woburn.

PAGE (see Paige), Abigail and Bowman Brown, Feb. 7, 1765.
Anna and Benjamin Lane, Dec. 9, 1779.

PAGE, Benjamin and Mary C. Worcester, Apr. 7, 1836.
Daniel [and] Abigail Jones, Oct. 10, 1765, in Concord.
David and Eliza S. Worcester, Apr. 2, 1835.
Dolly and Issachar Stearns, Sept. 16, 1796, in Billerica.
Dorcas and James Wright Jr., Mar. 16, 1797.
Ebenezer and Dorothy Fasset, Feb. 21, 1760. [Fassett, M.R.]
Ebenezer and Susanna Simonds [dup. Symonds], Dec. 4, 1781, in Woburn.
Elizabeth and Micah Reed, Dec. 3, 1772, in Lexington.
Esther B. and Asa Reed, Nov. 13, 1817.
Hannah and Jonas French, Jan. 5, 1758.
Joanna and Samuel Reed, July 25, 1771, in Lexington.
John [and] Mary Hartwell, Dec. 31, 1730, in Concord.
John and Amittai Fasset, Jan. 15, 1756, in Lexington.
John and Rachel Fitch, June 3, 1773.
John and Esther Merriam [dup. Meriam], Feb. 14, 1792. [Meriam, M.R.]
John of Dunstable, N.H., and Lucy Fitch, June 5, 1810.
Joshua and Salley [Sally, C.R.] Davis, July 15, 1802.
Joshua and Betsey May, Nov. 20, 1828.
Joshua and Mary Ann Robbins, Apr. 19, 1832.
Larkin P. and Rebecca Hunt, Dec. 3, 1829.
Lucy and Mather Hayward, May 1, 1800.
Margaret and Asa Fasset, Nov. 13, 1777.
Mary and Nathan Reed, Apr. 30, 1772, in Lexington.
Mary Ann and Orville Tyler, Mar. 16, 1834.
Moses and Hannah Putnam, Mar. 31, 1825.
Nathaniel Jr. and Sarah Brown, Dec. 15, 1774, in Lexington.
Nath[anie]l Jr. and Lydia Fitch, Sept. 10, 1801.
Phidela and Hiram Webber, July 20, 1824.
Polly and Seth Willson, May 8, 1794, in Billerica.
Rebekah and Solomon Cutler, Feb. 23, 1762, in Lexington.
Rebekah and Jonathan Willson, July 22, 1784.
Ruhamah and Jonathan Lane, July 27, 1815.
Sarah and Josiah Beard, Dec. 29, 1784.
Sarah and Samuel Randall, Nov. 27, 1806. [Randal, C.R.]
Susan and Samuel Bridge, Apr. 9, 1734. [Susanna Paige, C.R.]
Susanna and Amos Hagget, Jan. 16, 1781.
Susanna and John Webber, Nov. 21, 1786.
Susanna S., 24, d. William and Lucy, and Albion S. Willard, Apr. 9, 1848.
Thomas and Anna Merriam, Jan. 1, 1756, in Lexington.
Thomas Jr. and Betsey Porter, Nov. 26, 1807.
William and Patte Hill, Dec. 8, 1763, in Billerica.

PAIGE (see Page), Christopher and Susanna Webber, Feb. 2, 1742. [1742-3, C.R.]
Hannah and Rev. Reed Paige, Dec. 25, 1794.
Joanna and Josiah Fasset, Apr. 14, 1747.
Nathaniel Sr. and Mary Grimes, June 23, 1748. [Nathanael, C.R.] [Page, M.R.]
Reed, Rev. of Hancock, N.H., and Hannah Paige, Dec. 25, 1794.
Samuel of Ring, and Molly Hutchinson, Nov. 23, 1775. [Page of Ringe, M.R.]

PAINE, Nathaniel and Anna Robinson, Oct. 11, 1827.

PARKER, Benjamin of Chelmsford, and Sarah Lane, wid., July 14, 1791.
Benjamin and Sally Allen, June 28, 1801.
Daniel of Reading, and Mary Abbot, Aug. 4, 1774.
Molle and Heman Richardson, June 1, 1790. [Molly, and Haman Richardson, June 9, M.R.]
Robert [of] Reading, [and] Sarah Woolley, June 19, 1759, in Concord.
Sarah and Benjamin Danforth, July 7, 1748.
Stephen of Billerica, and Polly Duren, Jan. 30, 1791.

PARKHURST (see Parkhust), Jephthah and Mary Elizabeth Lane, Apr. 13, 1837.
Joseph of Wilton, and Rhoda Wyman, Nov. 26, 1807.
Samuel of Chelmsford, and Ann Dutton, Nov. 27, 1817.

PARKHUST (see Parkhurst), Samuel of Chelmsford, and Bette Hutchinson, Feb. 12, 1788. [Parkhurst, and Betty Hutchenson, M.R.]

PATTEN, Isaac and Lydia Chamberlain, Sept. 16, 1760, in Chelmsford.
Sophia and Francis Litchfield, Oct. 10, 1841.

PEIRCE (see Pierce), Susan, 23, d. George and Mare, and Walter E. Jewett, Dec. 19, 1848.

PENNIMAN, Joseph, Rev., and Mrs. Hannah Jackson, Oct. 10, 1771, in Plymouth.

PERRY, James [of] Concord, [and] Hannah Pollard, Mar. 30, 1764, in Concord.
Lucy and Thomas Harrington, July 4, 1771, in Lexington.

PHELPS, Joshua of Andover, and Dolly Watson, Apr. 18, 1822.
Lorenzo, 31, b. Wilton, N.H., s. Joseph and Anna of Wilton, N.H., and Susannah Cutting, wid., Sept. 5, 1847.
Timothy of Dedham, and Dorcas Chamberlain, Oct. 28, 1823.

PHILLIPS, Hepsibah and Jacob Bemis, Nov. 26, 1788, in Waltham.

PIERCE (see Peirce), Augustus and Mrs. Ruth E. Abbott, Nov. 15, 1835.
Mary, Mrs., and Ebenezer Hayward, Mar. 27, 1832.
Mary, 23, d. George and Mary, and Joshua Jackson, Nov. 28 [1844].
Ruth E., wid., 26, d. John Atwood and Margaret, and Thomas G. Butters, Sept. 9, 1846.

PIPER, Daniel B. and Elizabeth Carey, Dec. 1, 1836.

POLLARD, Betty and Joseph Loring Jr., Nov. 26, 1772, in Lexington.
David and Patte Dutton, Dec. 13, 1764.
Dorithy and Joseph Fasset, May 6, 1756. [Dorothy, and Joseph Fassett, M.R.]
Hannah [and] James Perry, Mar. 30, 1764, in Concord.
Hannah Elizabeth and Edward Winship, Jan. 22, 1839.
Jane and Thomas Smith, May 9, 1833.
Jonathan and Sarah Hagget [dup. Haggit], May 11, 1762.
Mary and Rev. William Gragg, Jan. 29, 1833.
Matthew and Elizabeth Lane, May 8, 1800.
Molley and James Lane, June 6, 1805.
Olive and Samuel Davis, Nov. 21, 1771.
Oliver and Hannah Hill, Feb. 17, 1735–6, in Billerica.
Oliver and Mrs. Susanna Richardson, July 22, 1762.
Oliver and Mary Hill, June 19, 1777, in Billerica.

PONT, James and Lucy Gardner Lun, Feb. 28, 1793, in Lunenburg.

POOL, Ruth and Castalio [Castatio, C.R.] Hosmer, Dec. 19, 1805.
Ruth and Jesse Reed, Oct. 28, 1819.

PORTER, Asa and Mary Mullikin, June 17, 1817.
Betsey and Thomas Page Jr., Nov. 26, 1807.
Desire and Abraham Brown, Sept. 21, 1774, in Concord.
Edith and William Caldwell, July 2, 1780.
Joseph Jr. of Danvers, and Ruth Hartwell, June 3, 1788.
Lucy and Samuel Sage, Jan. 1, 1815.

PORTER, Lydia and Benjamin Trask, Dec. 20, 1781.
Martha and Bradley Varnum Bowers, Aug. 24, 1817.
Mary and Stephen Bacon, Nov. 28, 1799.
Olive and Simon Hadley, Jan. 27, 1791. [Jan. 30, M.R.]
Rebecca P. and Thompson Bacon Jr., Apr. 17, 1821.
Sally and Israel Porter Hadley, July 14, 1816.
Sarah and David Wooly, June 16, 1774. [Worley, M.R.]
William of Concord, and Rebekah Willson, Apr. 4, 1799. [Wilson, C.R.]
William and Lucy F. Libbe, May 4, 1779.

POWERS, Edward of Boston, and Lois Fitch, Nov. 21, 1776.
John of Boston, and Louisa Crosby, Sept. 29, 1822.

PRATT, Martha and Constantine Hill, Nov. 7, 1835.

PREESE, Elizabeth and Edward Gardner, Feb. 29, 1776. [Elisabeth Preose, Feb. 19, M.R.]

PRENTICE, Will[ia]m of Sutton, and Abigail Willson, Oct. 29, 1754, in Woburn.

PRESCUT, Casas of Concord, and Jane Clark, negroes, May 18, 1780.

PRESTON, Amariah, Dr., and Hannah Reed, Oct. 28, 1790.
Amariah, Dr., and Ruhamah Lane, May 15, 1796.
Ezekiel W., and Lucy M. Stearns, May 18, 1823.
Susanna of New Ipswich, N.H., and Francis B. Maxwell, Mar. 19, 1812.

PRIEST, Aaron and Martha Bacon, May 7, 1782. M.R.
Nathan of Harvard, and Mary Bacon, July 5, 1780, in Bolton.

PROCTER (see Proctor), Hannah and David Fitch Jr., Nov. 12, 1799.

PROCTOR (see Procter), Hannah of Westford, and John Tidd Wright, Oct. 11, 1796, in Westford.
Mary and Jonathan Hill, Dec. 13, 1798, in Billerica.

PULSIFER, Robert S. of Boston, and Betsey Sprague, July 16, 1818.

PUTNAM, Benjamin and Eunice Reed, June 25, 1761.
Bridget and Jeremiah Rea, July 8, 1762.
Elijah and Lucy Webber, Apr. 28, 1803.
Elijah of Amherst, N.H., and Hannah Lane, Sept. 27, 1838.

PUTNAM, Elizabeth of Woburn, and Joseph Willson, June 18, 1745.
Elizabeth and Elisha Fuller, Nov. 28, 1752. [Elisabeth, C.R. M.R.]
Hannah and Moses Page, Mar. 31, 1825.
Israel Jr. and Sarah Hutchinson, Jan. 3, 1748–9.
Jonas of Roxbury, and Hannah Evans, Mar. 14, 1811.
Jonathan [and] Hannah Melvin, Aug. 21, 1750, in Concord.
Jonathan of Ringe [Rindge, M.R.], and Lucy Lane, Nov. 23, 1775.
Mary and John Jacobs, June 19, 1760.
Rebecca [and] Timothy Jones, Nov. 1, 1768, in Concord.
Rebekah and Eleazer Davis, Feb. 23, 1764.
Sarah and Matthew [Mathew, M.R.] Whipple, Apr. 4, 1751.

QUIMBY, Dyer and Rebekah Robinson, May 26, 1819.
Dyer of Boston, and Sarah Robinson, Sept. 27, 1821.

RANDALL, Samuel of Quincy, and Sarah Page, Nov. 27, 1806. [Randal, C.R.]

RANKINS, Margaret and James Chambers, May 13, 1742.

RAYMOND, Elizabth and Josiah Davis, Sept. 2, 1736. [Elizabeth, C.R.]
Hannah and David Reed, Jan. 28, 1772.
Mary and Stephen Heartwel, Dec. 31, 1741. [Heartwell, C.R.]
William and Marcy [Mercy, C.R.] Davis, Oct. 9, 1745.

REA, Eame [? Ame] and Amos Goodell, June 3, 176[ ]. [Anne, June 3, 1762, M.R.]
Jeremiah and Bridget Putnam, July 8, 1762.

REED, Abigail M. and Obadiah P. Johnson, Jan. 3, 1833.
Ann W. and Thomas Stiles, Apr. 11, 1838.
Asa and Naby Eames, Feb. 17, 1803. [Meads, and Nabby Eames, C.R.]
Asa and Esther B. Page, Nov. 13, 1817.
Benjamin and Sally Pollard Danforth, Apr. 17, 1817.
Benjamin of Lexington, and Bethiah L. Webber, Feb. 3, 1825.
Betsey and Rodney Clement, Apr. 28, 1835.
David and Hannah Raymond, Jan. 28, 1772.
David, Lt., and Abigail Simonds, Dec. 9 [dup. Dec. 28], 1791, in Woburn.
David, Capt., and Martha Simonds, Mar. 28, 1804.
David and Abigail Prince Danforth, Apr. 23, 1812.
David, 28, s. Benj[amin] and Sally, and Sarah Butters, Apr. 15, 1848.

REED, Eliot and Charles Gragg, Nov. 15, 1821.
Elizabeth and Moses Dunsmore, Feb. 13, 1794, in Acton.
Emely and Eleazer P. Davis, Mar. 15, 1831.
Emely Ann and Charles P. Robbins, Apr. 4, 1839.
Ephraim and Augusta Tarbell, Apr. 13, 1841.
Eunice and Benjamin Putnam, June 25, 1761.
Hannah and John Nutting, July 10, 1754, in Woburn.
Hannah and Dr. Amariah Preston, Oct. 28, 1790.
Hannah and Joseph Colburn, May 26, 1807.
Hannah and Warren Swain, Sept. 21, 1820.
Hannah Malvina Swain and Sylvanus Lawrence, Nov. 6, 1839.
Jesse and Ruth Pool, Oct. 28, 1819.
John Jr. and Hannah Merriam [dup. Meriam], Dec. 1, 1785. [Meriam, M.R.]
Louisa and Elbridge Bacon, Apr. 27, 1823.
Lucy P., d. Benj[amin] and w., and Elbridge Hartwell, Nov. 1, 1843.
Mary and Abner Ball, Apr. 30, 1789.
Mary of Lexington, and John Merriam [dup. Meriam], Dec. 3, 1799, in Lexington.
Mary and Abner Wheeler, Apr. 20, 1820.
Micah of Woburn, and Elizabeth Page, Dec. 3, 1772, in Lexington.
Nabby and William Colburn, May 28, 1816.
Nathan of Lexington, and Mary Page, Apr. 30, 1772, in Lexington.
Nathan O. and Martha S. Fitch, Dec. 18, 1834.
Nathan O. and Mrs. Nancy Fitch, Nov. 10, 1843.
Nathaniel of Lexington, and Hepsibah Bateman, Jan. 16, 1772, in Lexington.
Oliver Jr. and Bette Abbott, May 18, 1786. [Betty Abbot, M.R.]
Oliver Jr. and Mary Fitch, Sept. 2, 1810.
Polly and Jonathan Lawrence, Apr. 12, 1798, in Lexington.
Poulter and Molley [Molly, M.R.] Hartwell, Sept. 1, 1789.
Reuben of Lexington, and Salle Barrar, Aug. 28, 1782. [Sally Barrer, M.R.]
Robert of Woburn, and Elizabeth Hartwell, Mar. 2, 1771, in Lexington.
Roger and Sarah Webber, Nov. 25, 1790.
Ruhamah and John Lane " Tertiary " [*tertius*], Nov. 25, 1773, in Lexington.
Salley and Alford Fitch, June 4, 1818.
Samuel of Woburn, and Joanna Page, July 25, 1771, in Lexington.

REED, Samuel and Harriat Hodgman, May 12, 1825.
Sarah and Stephen Hartwell, Jan. 19, 1775, in Lexington.
Sarah and Ezra Groves, Sept. 14 [1813].
Susan and Albert Bacon, June 2, 1825.
William of Lexington, and Elizabeth Davis, Dec. 1, 1768, in Lexington.
William D., s. Benja[min] and w., and Lydia [dup. adds S.] Butters, Apr. 20, 1843.

RICE, David and Nancy Robbins, Jan. 31, 1822.
Dorcas and Alexander Mann, Mar. 25, 1838.
Harriot and Stephen Hull, Nov. 18 [1841].
Sarah and Oliver A. Wilson, Dec. 22, 1831.

RICHARDSON, Amity of Billerica, and Ebenezer Willson, Feb. 4, 1747, in Billerica.
Bartholomew 3d of Woburn, and Sally Richardson, May 29, 1794, in Woburn.
Ebenezer and Elizabeth Bacon, May 21, 1733, in Billerica.
Ebenezer of Billerica, and Susanna Davis, Nov. 23, 1790.
Hannah of Billerica, and Benjamin Kidder, Nov. 9, 1731, in Billerica.
Heman and Molle Parker, June 1, 1790. [Haman, and Molly Parker, June 9, M.R.]
John of Billerica, and Nabby Bacon, June 2, 1794, in Billerica.
Mary and Timothy Farley [Jr., C.R.], Oct. 17, 1743.
Sally and Bartholomew Richardson 3d, May 29, 1794, in Woburn.
Samuel of Woburn, and Lydia A. Mead, May 29, 1832.
Sarah W. and Artemas Webber, May 20, 1827.
Susanna, Mrs., of Billerica, and Oliver Pollard, July 22, 1762.
Wyle of Westford, and Mary Willson, Feb. 1, 1816.

RIPLEY, William 3d of Abington, and Abigail Bacon, Mar. 14, 1833.

ROBBINS, Charles P. and Emely Ann Reed, Apr. 4, 1839.
Joseph of Acton, and Ruth Bacon, Apr. 18, 1751.
Mary Ann of Acton, and Joshua Page, Apr. 19, 1832.
Nancy and David Rice, Jan. 31, 1822.
Perley of Boston, and Nancy Willson, Jan. 23 [1814].

ROBERSON (see Robinson), David of Ashburnham, and Susannah Wyman, Sept. 17, 1776. [Robinson of Ashburnham, Worcester Co., and Susanna Wyman, M.R.]

ROBINSON (see Roberson), Anna and Nathaniel Paine, Oct. 11, 1827.

ROBINSON, Daniel of New Ipswich, and Elizabeth Bacon, June 4, 1794.
Rebekah and Dyer Quimby, May 26, 1819.
Sarah and Dyer Quimby, Sept. 27, 1821.

ROGERS, Zebediah of Billerica, and Sarah Hutchinson, May 4, 1790.

ROLFE, Daniel of Billerica, and Abigel Herington, June 11, 1746. [Abigail Harrington, C.R. M.R.]

ROLLINS, Valintine P. and Lydia Brown, Apr. 6, 1837.

ROSE, Daniel and Acsak Ball, June 25, 1747, in Springfield.

ROSS, Mary and Abner Wheeler, Oct. 10, 1785.

RUSSELL, Ephriam of Lexington, and Mary Ann Wheeler, Jan. 9, 1755, in Lexington.
Harriot and Henry A. Young, July 15, 1840.
Jabez and Hannah Wheeler, Sept. 29, 1751. [Sept. 19, C.R. M.R.]
James C. and Mary Miller, Dec. 12, 1826.
John and Sally Bryant, Mar. 30, 1835.
Lucy and Eleazer Fisher, Jan. 1, 1829.
William and Salla Simonds, Aug. 17, 1797, in Chelmsford.

SAGE, Samuel and Lucy Porter, Jan. 1, 1815.

SALISBURY, William and Mrs. Sarah Wilson, Aug. 11, 1839.

SAMPSON, Polley and Ebenezer Clark, Sept. 15, 1805. [Polly, C.R.]

SANDERSON, George F., s. George, and Harriet L. Webber, July 15, 1849.

SAYLES, Susan M. and Eleazer P. Davis, Apr. 7, 1842.

SCHAFFER (see Shaffer), Eliza and Samuel Dexter, Aug. 26, 1824.

SCOTT, Samuel E., 25, of Westford, s. Samuel and w., and Loiza E. Forbush, May 12, 1844.

SHAFFER (see Schaffer), Mary Vila and Gardner Ball, June 30, 1825.

SHAW, Samuel D. and Nancy Vila, Apr. 15, 1819.

SHED, Abel of Stoddard, N.H., and Sophia Goodrige, Dec. 9, 1819.

SHERMAN, Nathaniel, Rev., and Mrs. Lydia Meriam, Mar. 1, 1759. [Shearman, M.R.]

SHORT, Thomas W. of Cambridge, and Elizabeth Wells, Mar. 5, 1820.

SIMONDS (see Simons), Abigail of Leominster, and Bezaliel Lawrence, Feb. 12, 1786, in Leominster.
Abigail of Woburn, and Lt. David Reed, Dec. 9 [dup. Dec. 28], 1791, in Woburn.
Abigail and John Boa [Ichabod, C.R.] Winchester, July 23, 1797.
Amittai and Daniel Flag, Nov. 1, 1832.
Benja[min] and Sarah Willson, June 11, 1744.
Bethiah and Hiram Whitford, Mar. 31, 1842.
Hannah and Joseph Trask, June 10, 1772, in Woburn.
James of Woburn, and Abigail Bacon, July 26, 1739.
James of Woburn, and Elizabeth Hall, June 30, 1763, in Lexington.
John and Abigail Heartwell, Jan. 9, 1766.
John and Jane D. Gibson, July 31, 1828.
Lucretia and David Bacon, Jan. 3, 1771, in Lexington.
Martha and Capt. David Reed, Mar. 28, 1804.
Nathan of Burlington, and Rachel Crosby, May 21, 1818.
Olive and David Fitch Jr., Jan. 8, 1805, in Burlington.
Rebeckah and Thomas Danforth, Sept. 19, 1734, in Billerica.
Rebeckah and Samuel Tidd, Feb. 28, 1771, in Lexington.
Salla and William Russell, Aug. 17, 1797, in Chelmsford.
Sarah and Benjamin Stratton, May 24, 1750.
Sarah of Lexington, and Francis Bowman, June 24, 1756, in Lexington.
Susanna [dup. Symonds] of Woburn, and Ebenezer Page, Dec. 4, 1781, in Woburn.
Zebedee and Amittai Webber, June 25, 1807.

SIMONS (see Simonds), Elizabeth and David Draper, Feb. 21, 1733-4. [Simonds, C.R.]
James and Lois Forbush, July 9, 1789, in Acton.

SKELTON (see Skilton), Benjamin, Dr., of Reading, and Iza Bacon, Oct. 18, 1810.
Daze and Ruth Hartwell, June 19, 1770, in Woburn.
Elias and Louisa Hartwell, Dec. 2, 1830.
Wyman of Burlington, and Dorcas Kendall, May 13, 1819.

SKILTON (see Skelton), John of Billerica, and Hannah Hartwell, June 4, 1805.

SKINNER, Joseph and Lydia S. Fitch, Dec. 10, 1837.
Martha and Eleazer Davis Jr., Jan. 1, 1799.
Sarah and James Marshall Jr., Apr. 9, 1816.
Susannah and Samson Spaulding, Mar. 27, 1804. [Susanna, and Sampson Spaulding, C.R.]

SLOAN, George W. and Dolly E. Wilson, July 26, 1832.

SMITH, Betty of Lexington, and Jonas Bacon, May 18, 1784, in Lexington.
Elizabeth, 21, d. John and Bethiah, and Moses F. Brown, Aug. 25 [1844].
Hanna of Lexington, and Timothy Davis, Feb. 9, 1736–7. [Hannah, C.R.]
Lucy D., d. John, and Silas F. Wild, Oct. 26, 1843.
Thomas and Jane Pollard, May 9, 1833.

SPAULDING (see Spawlding), Charles and Elizabeth C. Wilson, May 4, 1826.
Samson and Susannah Skinner, Mar. 27, 1804. [Sampson, and Susanna Skinner, C.R.]

SPAWLDING (see Spaulding), Ebenezer of Canterbury, and Mary Fasset, Feb. 24, 1742. [Spaulding, 1742–3, C.R.]

SPRAGUE (see Sprake), Betsey and Robert S. Pulsifer, July 16, 1818.
Susan and William Clark, Apr. 24, 1832.

SPRAKE (see Sprague), John and Phebe Fitch, Apr. 1, 1784. [July 22, 1784, M.R.]

STAPLES, Ebenezer of Mendon, and Mary Davis, Mar. 20, 1744–5.
Henry H. and Catherine Edwards, Dec. 8, 1836.

STARNS (see Stearns), Elizabeth and John Bacon, Dec. 20, 1744. [Stearns, C.R.]

STEARNS (see Starns), Abigail F. and Jonas Monroe, Nov. 24, 1831.
Abner, Lt., and Anna Hill, May 1, 1796.
Alise and Moses Abbot Jr., Dec. 7, 1786. [Alice, M.R.]
Charles and Lorinda Wilson, Mar. 30, 1828.
Edward [dup. Edwerd] [and] Polly Jones, Dec. 23, 1794, in Concord.
Edward, Lt., and Nabby Jones, Jan. 1, 1798.
Elbridge W. and Ruth T. Wright, Dec. 17, 1826.

STEARNS, Elijah of Billerica, and Lucy Lane, Dec. 20, 1759. [Feb. 20, 1760, M.R.]
Elijah and Elizabeth Stearns, Dec. 30 [1802].
Elizabeth and Elijah Stearns, Dec. 30 [1802].
Elizabeth W. and Dea. Charles James, Dec. 8, 1831.
Isaac of Billerica, and Sarah Abbott, Feb. 11, 1747-8. [Abbot, M.R.]
Issachar of Billerica, and Dolly Page, Sept. 16, 1796, in Billerica.
John of Billerica, and Polley [Polly, C.R.] Lane, Feb. 10, 1801.
Lucy M. and Ezekiel W. Preston, May 18, 1823.
Nabby and Rev. Ebenezer Hill, Sept. 22, 1799.
Rachel of Billerica, and Nathan Hutchinson, Apr. 16, 1741, in Billerica.
Sally M. and Stephen R. Niclass, Oct. 22, 1829.
Samuel of Billerica, and Elizabeth [Elisabeth, M.R.] Hutchinson, Oct. 31, 1749.
Samuel, Rev., and Abigail French, May 9, 1797, in Andover.
Sarah of Billerica, and Thaddeus Davis, Sept. 28, 1779, in Billerica.
Sarah and Solomon Lane, May 29, 1781.
Sarah Caroline and Rev. Forest Jefferds, Sept. 27, 1827.
Susannah H. and James C. Cotting, Jan. 3, 1841.
Timothy of Billerica, and Sarah Lane, Nov. 1, 1787.
William of Billerica, and Lydia Davis, Sept. 25, 1777.
William and Betsey Davis, Feb. 12, 1801.

STEPHENS (see Stevens), Lorenzo, 35, of Roxbury, s. Abel (Stevens) and Haddassah, and Mary G. P. Edland, Jan. 29, 1846.

STEVENS (see Stephens), Benjamin of Methuen, and Hannah Hall, Oct. 25, 1782.

STICKNEY, Elizabeth, Mrs., and Job Lane, Jan. 15, 1777.

STILES, Lucius and Lavinia Lawrence, Sept. 11, 1843.
Thomas and Ann W. Reed, Apr. 11, 1838.

STODDARD, Daniel of Boston, and Lydia Sewell Willson, Dec. 25, 1806.

STONE, Joseph of Framingham, and Rebekah Meriam, Jan. 13, 1758.

STOW, Nathan of Concord, and Polley Barrett, May 12, 1814.

STRATTON, Benjamin of Lexington, and Sarah Simonds, May 24, 1750.

SWAIN, Lucy and Dea. Michael Crosby, May 19, 1816, in Boston.
Warren of S. Reading, and Hannah Reed, Sept. 21, 1820.

SWEETSER, Seth of Woburn, and Dorcas C. Wright, Jan. 6, 1824.

TAILYOR (see Taylor), Abraham of Dunstable, and Lydia Whittacor, Jan. 21, 1730–2 [sic]. [Taylor, and Lydia Whitaker, 1730–1, C.R.]

TARBELL, Augusta and Ephraim Reed, Apr. 13, 1841.
Catherine, 28, d. Ziba and Betsey, and Josiah D. Brown, Apr. 10 [1845].
David of Billerica, and Hannah Fitch, Aug. 1, 1751.

TAYLOR (see Tailyor), David [and] Ruth Jones, Feb. 5, 1745, in Concord.
Hannah and John Wheeler, May 23, 1754.
Jonathan [and] Mary Jones, Aug. 29, 1754, in Concord.
Samuel, widr., b. Eng., s. ―― of Eng., and Ann Jane Lawhead, Feb. 8, 1843.

TEAL, Jane of Medford, and John Francis, June 3, 1777. [Teel, M.R.]

TEMPLE, Abigail and Nathaniel Hayden, Sept. 29, 1731, in Sudbury.

TEMPLETON, Jesse and Joanna Balch, Nov. 20, 1825.

THOMPSON, Abigail of Woburn, and William Fothingham, Oct. 20, 1805.
Abijah of Woburn, and Lydia Meeds, July 1, 1790.
Andrew of Windham, and Margaret Maxwell, June 30, 1756.

TIDD, Benjamin of Lexington, and Joanna Fitch, Jan. 6, 1774, in Lexington.
John of Woburn, and Sukey Davis, May 28, 1818.
Samuel of Lexington, and Rebeckah Simonds, Feb. 28, 1771, in Lexington.
Samuel of Woburn, and Mary Davis, Dec. 26, 1809.

TISDALE, James of Lexington, and Hannah Mead, Aug. 13, 1772. M.R.

TOWNS, Ellen of Andover, and Hiram L. Dutton, Apr. 4, 1843, in Andover.

TRASK, Benjamin of Lexington, and Lydia Porter, Dec. 20, 1781.
Cloe of Lexington, and David Fisk, Aug. 10, 1820.
Joseph of Woburn, and Hannah Simonds, June 10, 1772, in Woburn.

TUTTLE, Mary M., wid., 22, d. John and Susan, and Thomas G. Atkins, Oct. 12, 1848.

TWIST, Mary Ann and Benjamin A. Webber, Apr. 12, 1826.

TYLER, Orville of Concord, and Mary Ann Page, Mar. 16, 1834.

UNDERWOOD, Sarah and Josiah Upton, Mar. 21, 1782.

UPTON, Josiah and Sarah Underwood, Mar. 21, 1782.

VARNUM, Dorkes and Phinehas Chamberlin, Feb. 21, 1797, in Chelmsford.

VILA, Nancy and Samuel D. Shaw, Apr. 15, 1819.

WAIT, Mary and John Danforth, Mar. 24, 1763, in Lexington.

WALKER, Ezekiel and Amity Wilson, July 21, 1755, in Charlestown.

WALTON, Catherine and Oliver A. Lane, [July] 23, 1818.
Joshua and Hannah Dutton, Mar. 6, 1770, in Lexington.

WARE, Emeline A. and Joseph S. Newhall Jr., May 25, 1841.

WARREN, Cyrus of Concord, and Nancy Bacon, Dec. 16, 1819.

WATSON, Dolly and Joshua Phelps, Apr. 18, 1822.
Mary and Elijah Bacon, Jan. 26, 1823.

WATTS, Isaac L., 22, and Martha E. Hosmer, June 17, 1847.
Nathaniel P., s. Isaac and w., and Maria Hosmer, Oct. 12, 1843.

WAYMAN (see Wyman), Samuel and Abigail Center, Dec. 22, 1774. [Wyman, M.R.]

WEBBER, Amittai and Zebedee Simonds, June 25, 1807.
Artemas and Sarah W. Richardson, May 20, 1827.
Asa and Elliot [Eliot, C.R.] Reed Lane, Apr. 30, 1801.

WEBBER, Benjamin A. and Mary Ann Twist, Apr. 12, 1826.
Benjamin N. of Lowell, and Ann Win, Sept. 5, 1837.
Bethiah L. and Benjamin Reed, Feb. 3, 1825.
Betsey A. and George Wilson, Oct. 9, 1831.
Elizabeth B. and George Frazer, Nov. 19, 1826.
Harriet L., 20, d. Hiram and Fidelia, and George F. Sanderson, July 15, 1849.
Hiram of Boston, and Phidela Page, July 20, 1824.
James and Hannah Davis, Aug. 7, 1804.
Job and Sarah Davis, June 21, 1796.
John and Sarah Fasset, Apr. 10, 1760. [Fassett, M.R.]
John Jr. and Bethiah [Bethia, M.R.] Lane, Dec. 15, 1785.
John and Susanna Page, Nov. 21, 1786.
Joseph Jr. and Eliza Bacon, Jan. 10, 1819.
Lucy and Elijah Putnam, Apr. 28, 1803.
Lydia and Samuel Fletcher [Jr., C.R.], Apr. 18, 1805.
Lydia P. and David Clark, Feb. 21, 1839.
Sarah and Roger Reed, Nov. 25, 1790.
Susanna of Medford, and Christopher Paige, Feb. 2, 1742. [1742–3, C.R.]
Theresa E., 20, d. Joseph and Eliza, and Joseph Litchfield, Sept. 18, 1845.
William and Mary Abbot, May 10, 1791.
William and Mary W. Gleason, Oct. 11, 1835.

WELLINGTON, Anna and Eliab Banidge Lane, Mar. 21, 1802. [Willington, C.R.]
Cherry of Cambridge, and Capt. James Lane, Aug. 9, 1763, in Lexington.
Joseph Adams of Waltham, and Lucy Bacon, Mar. 25, 1798. [Willington, C.R.]
Mary and James Lane Jr., Jan. 10, 1750–1.

WELLS, Elizabeth and Thomas W. Short, Mar. 5, 1820.

WHEAT, Lois and Thomas C. Cutler, Apr. 14, 1840.

WHEELER (see Wheelor, Whellor), Abner and Mary Ross, Oct. 10, 1785.
Abner and Anna Davis, June 1, 1817.
Abner and Mary Reed, Apr. 20, 1820.
Benjamin of Concord, and Susanna Williams, Sept. 11, 1777, in Malden.
Catherine, 35, b. Acton, and Nathan[ie]l C. Cutler, widr., May 10, 1849.

WHEELER, David of Concord, and Sarah Meriam, Dec. 27, 1733. C.R.
Hannah and Jabez Russell, Sept. 29, 1751. [Sept. 19, C.R. M.R.]
Jacob, widr., 44, s. Abner and Mary, and Elizabeth Hovey, Nov. 24 [1844].
John and Hannah Taylor, May 23, 1754.
Lucy of Acton, and John Hodgman, Aug. 22, 1832.
Lydia and Benjamin Winship, Apr. 18, 1780.
Mary and John Moore Jr., July 17, 1759. [Moor, M.R.]
Mary Ann and Ephriam Russell, Jan. 9, 1755, in Lexington.
Olive and Nathaniel [Nathanael, C.R.] Meriam, Dec. 27, 1748.
Phinehas, Dea., of Acton, and Mrs. Elizabeth Hodgman, Sept. 15, 1831.
Richard and Eunice Davis, Dec. 15, 1743. C.R.
Richard and Mrs. Anne Bateman, Dec. 10, 1760.

WHEELOR (see Wheeler, Whellor), Jothom of Concord, and Sarah Bacon, Mar. 30, 1775. [Jonathan Wheeler, M.R.]

WHELLOR (see Wheeler, Wheeler), Elizabeth and John Moore, Sept. 4, 1740. [Wheeler, and John Moor, C.R.]

WHETNEE (see Whitney, Witney), Mary and William Grimes, Jan. 1, 1740–1. [Whitney, C.R.]

WHIPPLE, Matthew of Salem, and Sarah Putnam, Apr. 4, 1751. [Mathew, M.R.]

WHIT (see White), Nathan and Dorcas Lane, Jan. 3, 1788.

WHITCOMB, Abraham of Stow, and Dolley Hartwell, May 27, 1804.
Peter of Boxborough, and Sarah Wyman, Nov. 25 [1802].

WHITE (see Whit), Caleb Harrington and Hannah Gleason, June 28, 1799. [June 20, C.R.]
Dorcas and Benjamin Hubbard, Apr. 3, 1811.
Elizabeth and Aaron Willis, May 18, 1817.
Leonard and Mary An Burnam, Nov. 29, 1832.

WHITFORD, Hiram and Bethiah Simonds, Mar. 31, 1842.
Seth and Lydia Ann Manning, Feb. 19, 1835.
William and Sarah Bacon, Feb. 16, 1826.

WHITING, John of Littleton, and Ruth Lane, Dec. 29, 1772.

WHITMORE (see Whittemore, Whittomore), Jemima and William Howard, Mar. 9, 1782. [Hayward, M.R.]

WINSHIP, Richard of Lincoln, and Sale Farrel, Feb. 21, 1788. [Sally Turrel, M.R.]

WINSLOW, Annar and Benjamin Maxwell, Jan. 7, 1762. [Anna, M.R.]

WITNEY (see Whetnee, Whitney), Daniel of Stow, and Sarah Duron, Dec. 10, 1778.

WOLCOTT, Mary B. and Francis W. R. Emery, Mar. 26, 1839.

WOOD (see Woods), Dorcas and Joseph Moore, Feb. 22, 1753. [Dorothy, M.R.]
Dorothy and William Cary, May 24, 1755, in Concord.
Maria of Boston, and Thomas C. Cutler, Apr. 17, 1828.
Martha and Almond Fitch, Mar. 30 [1814].

WOODS (see Wood), Henry Jr. of Pepperil, and Alice Fitch, May 3, 1780.

WOODWARD, Daniel of Boston, and Lydia N. Wilson, Dec. 25, 1806. C.R.

WOOLLEY (see Wooly), Hannah and Zedekiah Drury, Apr. 2, 1741. C.R
John and Mary Blood, Apr. 30, 1754. [Wooley, M.R.]
Mary and John Fasset, May 14, 1741. [Fassett, C.R]
Mary and Josiah Davis, Apr. 26, 1764. [Wooley, M.R.]
Nathan [and] Sarah Flagg, Oct. 3, 1754, in Concord.
Sarah [and] Robert Parker, June 19, 1759, in Concord.

WOOLY (see Woolley), David and Sarah Porter, June 16, 1774. [Worley, M.R.]

WORCESTER, Eliza S. and David Page, Apr. 2, 1835.
Mary C. and Benjamin Page, Apr. 7, 1836.

WRIGHT, Betsey and Joseph Brown, Oct. 5, 1809.
Betsey and Edward Hoar, Nov. 29, 1827.
Dorcas C. and Seth Sweetzer, Jan. 6, 1824.
James Jr. and Dorcas Page, Mar. 16, 1797.
John Tidd and Hannah Proctor, Oct. 11, 1796, in Westford.
Mary L. and James Gibson, Apr. 17, 1831.
Ruth T. and Elbridge W. Stearns, Dec. 17, 1826.
Sarah and Abel S. Monroe, Apr. 26, 1838.

WYETH (see Wyrth).

WYLLIS (see Willis).

WYMAN (see Wayman), Elizabeth and Jonathan Bacon, Sept. 22, 1739, in Woburn.
Nathaniel Jr. and Elizabeth Bacon, Apr. 9, 1795, in Lexington.
Prisca and Benjamin Draper Jr., Nov. 14, 1816.
Rhoda and Joseph Parkhurst, Nov. 26, 1807.
Samuel and Sarah Corbin, Oct. 26, 1837.
Sarah and Peter Whitcomb, Nov. 25 [1802].
Sasanna and Thaddeus Dean, Mar. 16, 1786.
Susannah and David Roberson, Sept. 17, 1776. [Susanna, and David Robinson, M.R.]

WYRTH, Noah of Cambridge, and Betty Fitch, Mar. 30, 1763, in Lexington.

YOUNG, Henry A. and Harriot Russell, July 15, 1840.

YOURS, Susanna and Samuel Bathrick, Dec. 11, 1740. C.R.

BEDFORD DEATHS.

BEDFORD DEATHS.

To the year 1850.

ABBOT (see Abbott), Benjamin, s. Moses Jr. and Allice, Apr. 29, 1795. [Abbott, s. Moses and Alice, a. 1 y. 3 m., G.R.]
Betsey, d. Moses and Allis, Nov. 26, 1792.
Edward Stearns, s. Moses Jr. and Allice, Dec. 18, 1798. [worms, a. 22 m., C.R.] [Abbott, s. Moses Jr. and Alice, G.R.]
Eliza, d. Moses Jr. and Allice, June 4, 1802. ["cough which terminated in fits and pobably consumption," June 3, a. 5 m., C.R.]
Harvey, s. Moses Jr. and Allis, Mar. 28, 1789.
Moses Jr., Feb. 19, 1802, in 41st y. [consumption, a. 41, C.R.] [Abbott, G.R.]

ABBOTT (see Abbot), Benjamin, s. Capt. Moses and Mary, May 21, 1793. [in 28th yr., G.R.]
Benja[min] F. [dup. B. F.], s. Oliver R. [and] Mary Ann [dup. fits], June 23, 1842, a. 3 y. 11 m. 20 d. [dup. a. 1]
Elizabeth, w. Obed, May 29, 1752. [Abbot, C.R.] [in 59th y., G.R.]
John, Nov. 27, 1756, a. 23, "in ye army at Lake George." G.R.
Mary, w. Capt. Moses, Sept. 5, 1801. [Abbot, fever, a. 67, C.R.] [Sept. 5, 1807, a. 66, G.R.]
Mary Ann, d. James Wilson and Dolly, Dec. 26, 1825, a. 18 y. 7 m. 28 d. [w. Lt. Oliver, a. 19, G.R.]
Moses, Capt., Nov. 22, 1809, a. 83.
Obed, May 11, 1772, in 77th y. [May 11, 1773, G.R.]
Oliver R., consumption, Sept. 11, 1842, a. 43 [dup. 42 y. 11 m., 16 d.].
———, ch. Moses Jr. and Allice, still born, Dec. 5, 1798.

BACON, Abijah, s. John and Elizabeth, May 1, 1776, a. 22. G.R.
Alice, d. John O. and Clara A., dropsey on the brain, Mar. 5, 1848, a. 1 y. 5 m.
Alonzo [Bacon], s. Reuben Jr. and Ruth, Mar. 26, 1835.
Amittai, w. Benjamin, Oct. 10, 1806, a. 47 y. 8 m. 1 d. [consumption, a. 48, C.R.]

BACON, Benjamin, Dea., Oct. 1, 1791, a. 78.
Briget, d. Jonathan and Elizabeth, Apr. 20, 1731. [Bridget, C.R.] [Breget, a. 25, G.R.]
Catharine, d. Benj[amin] and Catharine, Mar. 5, 1754. [Katharine, C.R.]
Catharine, w. Dea. Benjamin, July 17, 1791, in 74th y. [Katherine, July 7, a. 74, G.R.]
Elbridge, m., s. Thompson and Martha, dropsey, Aug. 31, 1848, a. 48.
Elbridge, s. Thompson, Aug. 3, 1849.
Elijah, Sept. 13, 1788. [a. 34, G.R.]
Elizabeth, w. Jonathan, Dec. 16, 1738. [Dec. 15, C.R.] [a. 67, G.R.]
Elizabeth, d. John and Elizabeth, Aug. 26, 1749.
Elizabeth, d. John and Elizabeth, Feb. 15, 1754. [in 4th y., G.R.]
Emily Frances, d. Elbridge and Louisa, Dec. 31, 1838, a. 7. G.R.
Emily Frances, d. Edward and Charlotte, affection of the spine, Oct. 5, 1845, a. 2 y. 4 m.
Emma C., d. Clark and Emma C., Aug. 16, 1833, a. 2 m. 4 d. G.R.
Frederick W., s. Warren and Lucy, cancer, Sept. 5, 1846, a. 4 y. 4 m.
Hannah, w. John, Sept. 27, 1823, a. 70. G.R.
Isaac, s. Benjamin and Catharine, June 10, 1748. [June 13, C.R.]
Issac, s. Benj[amin] and Catharine, Mar. 16, 1754.
Isaac, s. Benjamin and Esther, July 18, 1778.
Iza, June 6, 1787, a. 8. G.R.
Jesse, s. John and Elizabeth, Aug. 21, 1749. [Aug. 25, C.R.] [Aug. 26, a. 19 d., G.R.]
Jesse, s. Benjamin and Esther, July 17, 1778.
Job Lane, s. Benja[min] Jr. and Martha, Sept. 9, 1805. [hooping cough, a. 14 m., C.R. [a. 13 m. 22 d., G.R.]
John, s. John and Elizabeth, Aug. 30, 1749. [a. 3, G.R.]
John, May 26, 1760, in 44th y.
John, June 7, 1833, a. 80. G.R.
Jonathan, Mr., Jan. 12, 1754. [a. 82, C.R.]
Joseph, Nov. 29, 1747. [in 63d y., G.R.]
Martha, [wid.] Thompson Esq., consumption, Feb. 15 [dup. Feb. 4], 1847, a. 84. [Feb. 13, G.R.]
Nathan, s. Michael, Sept. 7, 1745. C.R.
Nathan, Aug. 1, 1775.
Nathaniel, Dec. 7, 1747. C.R.
Octa, s. Thompson Esq. and Martha, July 28, 1811. [a. 16 y. 3 m., G.R.]

BACON, Oliver, ch. Oliver and Sarah, Apr. 17, 1787, a. 11. G.R.
Oliver, May 25, 1794, a. 54. G.R.
Rebekah, d. Joseph and Rebekah, Feb. 20, 1763.
Rebekah, wid. Joseph, Aug. 24, 1778, a. 91 y. 1 m. 16 d.
Reuben, s. John and Elizabeth, May 15, 1775, in 18th y. [May 22, G.R.]
Reuben, s. Thompson and Martha, Dec. 20, 1785.
Rhoda, d. Benj[amin] and Catharine, Dec. 9, 1757.
Ruth, w. Reuben Jr., July 19, 1838, a. 24. G.R.
Sarah, d. Joseph and Rebeca, Feb. 16, 1730-1. [Feb. 17, C.R.]
Sarah, w. Mical, Apr. 17, 1745. [w. Michael, C.R.]
Sarah, first d. Benj[amin] Jr. and Marcha, Sept. 19, 1799. [canker rash, Sept. 17, a. 5, C.R.] [Sept. 17, G.R.]
Sarah, wid. Oliver, Jan. 25, 1841, in 94th y. G.R.
Susanna, d. Michael and Elizabeth, ———.
Thompson Esq., Dec. 4, 1833, a. 73.
Thompson, s. Thompson Esq. and Martha, Mar. 19, 1838, a. 40.
Warren, s. Jonathan and Abigail, Jan. 28, 1822. [a. 6 y. 15 d., G.R.]
William, Aug. 21, 1775.
———, inf. s. Samuel, Feb. 24, 1748-9. C.R.
———, inf. s. John, May 8, 1752. C.R.
———, w. Capt. Flag, consumption, June 7, 1800, a. 30. C.R.
———, youngest ch. Flag, Apr. 7, 1801, a. 2 y. 6 m., in Lexington. C.R.

BALCH, Elizabeth, Mrs., Jan. 31, 1736-7. C.R. [w. Freeborn of Beverly, G.R.]

BALLARD, Joseph, Dr., Jan. 29, 1777.

BARNEY, Daniel, Apr. 7, 1736. C.R.

BARRETT, Frederick, s. William and Helen A., cholera infantum, Aug. 10, 1848, a. 5 m. 4 d.

BATEMAN, Sarah, wid., Jan. 15, 1739-40, a. 95. C.R.

BEARD, Sam[ue]l of Vermont, nervous fever, May 1, 1797, a. abt. 20. C.R.

BIGELOW, Emma Louisa, b. Abington, d. Prescott J. and Eliza Ann, erysipilas, July 20, 1849, a. 5 y. 3 m.
Frederick P., s. Prescott J. and Eliza Ann, erysipelas, Aug. 28, 1849, a. 2 y. 8 m.

BILLINGS, Lucy, Oct. 28, 1838, a. 64. G.R.

BLANCHARD, Isaac, b. Carlisle, s. Benj[a]m[in] and Martha, typhus fever, Oct. 26, 1844, a. 26.

BLODGET, ———, ch. Simeon, Aug. 28, 1807, a. 1 hr. c.r.

BLOOD, Abraham, s. Jeremiah and Sarah, Aug. 8, 1778.
Daniel Hartwell, s. Jeremiah and Sarah, Sept. 4, 1791, in 27th y.

BOWES, Thomas, s. Rev. Nicholas and Lucy, May 21, 1750. [May 25, c.r.] [May 21, a. 2 y. 11 m., g.r.]

BOWMAN, Jonas, June 5, 1783, in 67th y.
Mary, d. Francis and Sarah, Nov. 20, 1762. g.r.
———, Mr., mortification, Dec. 6, 1797, a. "above 70." c.r.

BROWN, Betsey, w. Joseph, June 30, 1818, a. 29.
John, s. Nathaniel and Ruth, Sept. 12, 1805. [Sept. 12, 1803, a. 5, g.r.]
Joseph, Dec. 23, 1762, a. 29 y. 1 m. [Dec. 25, a. 30, g.r.]
Joseph, s. Nath[anie]l, dysentery, Sept. 12, 1805, a. 5. c.r.
———, Dea. of Gerry, fever, Dec. 24, 1802. c.r.

BUTLER, Samuel, disease of the spine [and] consumption, May 10, 1847, a. 49.

BUTTERFIELD, ———, ch. Charles, July —, 1842, a. 3 m.

BUTTRICK, Willard, m., b. Concord, palsey, July 25, 1849, a. 77 y. 11 m. 15 d.
———, d. Willard and w., Aug. 10, 1843, a. 3 m.

CALDWELL, Mary, d. Adam, Feb. 9, 1754. c.r.
Ruth, d. Adam, Feb. 1, 1754. c.r.
———, inf. d. Adam, May 9, 1752. c.r.
———, ch. John, fits, June 21, 1803, a. 5 d. c.r.

CAREY, James, s. James (Cary), Jan. 13, 1735–6. c.r.

CHAMBERLIN, Dorcas, wid., old age, Mar. 5, 1849, a. 76.
Henry, s. Phinehas W. and Esther, croup, May 9, 1849, a. 4 y. 6 m. 27 d.
Phinehas, s. Phineas W. and Esther, dysentery, Sept. 24, 1847, a. 5 m.
Phinehas, s. Phinehas and Esther, cholera infantum, Oct. 15, 1848, a. 6 m. 12 d.
———, ch. Phin[ea]s, still born, Feb. 22, 1805. c.r.

CHEEVER (see Chever), Daniel, s. Daniel and Ruth, July 7, 1747, in 21st y.

CHEVER (see Cheever), Daniel, July 10, 1733, in 40th y. [Cheever, July 11, C.R.]
Ruth, wid. Danel, Feb. 7, 1735–6, in 44th y. [Cheever, C.R.]

CLARK, Samuel, s. William and Susan, fever, Sept. 8, 1846, a. 3.
———, ch. Leander and Laura, inflamation of lungs, Mar. 1, 1848.

COLBOURN, Benjamin, July 10, 1746. C.R.

CONVASS (see Convers), John, Apr. 26, 1783, a. 7 d.

CONVERS (see Convass), Sarah, d. William and Sarah, Apr. 13, 1803. [Converse, Apr. 11, a. 9 hrs., C.R.]

COOPER, Caroline, w. William H., consumption, Mar. 11, 1846, a. 43.

CORBET (see Corbit).

CORBIN, ———, ch. Stephen, sore mouth, Mar. 8, 1805, a. 17 d. C.R.

CORBIT, James, s. John, Apr. 6, 1745. C.R.

COTTING, James, b. Marlborough, consumption, Nov. 24, 1843, a. 26.
Mary Louisa, d. John R. and Emaline H., cholera infantum, Sept. 13, 1849, a. 5 m. 2 w.
Sarah C., w. John R., child bed, Mar. 3, 1848, a. 29. [Cutting, G.R.]

CRAWFORD, Thomas, s. Thomas and Caroline, July 22, 1846, a. 7.
———, ch. Tho[ma]s, May —, 1842.

CROSBY, Artemas, s. Dea. Michael and Asenath, May 27, 1814.
Asenath, d. Dea. Michael and Asenath, June 24, 1811.
Asenath, w. Dea. Michael, Apr. 23, 1812, a. 44.
Franklin, s. Dea. Michael and Asenath, Dec. 12, 1819.

CUTLER, Louisa Maria, d. Thomas C. and Lois, cholera infantum, May 14, 1848, a. 3 y. 2 m. 2 d.
Sarah, w. Samuel, consumption, May 14, 1844, a. 40.
Susan E., w. Nathaniel C., consumption, Feb. 4, 1847, a. 39.

CUTTING (see Cotting).

DANFORTH, Benjamin, Dec. 31, 1808, a. 82 y. 5 m.

DAVIS, Aaron, s. Stephen and Elizabeth, Nov. 3, 1727.
Almira, b. Ashburnham, d. Paul and w., dropsy, Aug. 8, 1844, a. 14.
Daniel, Mr., Feb. 10, 1740–1. [a. 67, G.R.]
Ebenezer, s. Stephen and Elizabeth, Aug. 30, 1754.
Eleazar, Sept. 12, 1748, in 43d y.
Eleazer, Lt., Mar. 13, 1819, a. 85. G.R.
Elizabeth, d. Eleazar and Rebckah, Feb. 6, 1749–50. [d. Rebekah, wid., C.R.]
Elizabeth, w. Josiah, Jan. 15, 1763. [a. 41, G.R.]
Elizabeth, w. Dea. Stephen, Dec. 5, 1789, a. 71 y. 2 m. 20 d.
Ezra, s. Daniel and Mary, ———, 1721, a. 10 w.
Hannah, d. Daniel and Mary, Apr. 11, 1738. [Apr. 10, C.R.] [Apr. 11, 1737, a. 14 y. 2 m. 21 d., G.R.]
Hannah, d. Stephen and Elizabeth, Aug. 31, 1754.
Isaac L., Ens., Nov. 8, 1817, a. 24, in New Orleans.
John, s. Stephen and Elizabeth, Feb. 14, 1739–40.
Jonas, s. Stephen and Elizabeth, Sept. 25, 1723.
Jonathan, s. Josiah and Elizabeth, May 2, 1750.
Joshua, Apr. 29, 1746. C.R. [a. 31, G.R.]
Marcy, d. Daniel and Mary, Nov. 4, 1709.
Martha Joanna, d. Eleazer Jr. and Martha, ———. [Feb. 10, 1817, in 9th y., G.R.]
Mary, w. Eleazer, Jan. 28, 1763. [a. 22 y. 10 m. 2 d., G.R.]
Mary, d. Simon and Allice, Oct. 4, 1813.
Mary, dispeptia, Jan. —, 1843, a. 39.
Paul, s. Josiah and Elizabeth, Jan. 12, 1763. [Jan. 9, a. 17, G.R.]
Phillip, s. Stephen and Elizabeth, June 11, 1719.
Phillip Jr., s. Stephen and Elizabeth, Mar. 10, 1728.
Rebekah, w. Lt. Eleazer, ———. G.R.
Ruth, d. Stephen and Elizabeth, Feb. 29, 1728.
Samuel, s. Stephen and Elizabeth, May 2, 1729.
Samuel, s. Eleazar and Rebekah, Feb. 17, 1749–50.
Sarah, w. Dea. Thaddeus, May 26, 1807, a. 48. [consumption, C.R.] [Mar. 26, a. 47, G.R.]
Simon, May 20, 1815, a. 31.
Stephen, July 11, 1738, in 53d y. [suddenly, C.R.] [a. 53, G.R.]
Stephen, Dea., July 22, 1787. [a. 71, G.R.]
———, ch. Thad[deu]s, dysentery, Dec. 10, 1796, a. 7 m. C.R.
———, ch. Daniel, fits, June 14, 1804, a. 4 d C.R.
———, d. T. H. and w., Apr. 3, 1844, a. 1.

DEAN, Benjamin, Mr., Mar. 22, 1767.
Elizabeth, w. Thaddeus, June 7, 1785, a. 37.

DEAN, Joseph, Mr., Mar. 4, 1744–5. [Mar. 3, C.R.]
Supply, d. Thaddeus and Susanna, Dec. 10, 1796.
Supply, May 25, 1826, a. 26. G.R.
Thaddeus, s. Thaddeus and Elizabeth, June 29, 1787.
Thaddeus, consumption, Dec. 3, 1803, a. 55. C.R.
———, ch. Thad[deu]s, dysentery, Oct. 1, 1801, a. 5 m. C.R.

DRURY, Hannah, w. Zedekiah, Jan. 11, 1739–40 [*sic*, see birth rec. of Zedekiah].

DUDLEY, Hanna, w. Silas, Aug. 1, 1828, a. 27. G.R.

DUTTON, Ellen F., d. Hiram L. and Ellen, merasmus, Nov. 8, 1847, a. 6 m.
Excy Maria, d. George and Lydia, typhus fever, July 5, 1849, a. 16 y. 8 m. 12 d.
Sarah, d. David and Hannah, Sept. 26, 1761.

EDWARDS, Rachel Ann, d. Rowert W. and Emaline, cholera infantum, Sept. 21, 1849, a. 6 m. 26 d.

ELWELL, David, m., b. Standish, Me., s. Isaac and Mary, scrofulor and dropsy, Mar. 16, 1845, a. 47 y. 10 m. 23 d.

EVANS, ———, Mrs., paralytic shock, May 4, 1800, a. 39. C.R.

EVERETT, William, s. William and Anna, June 11, 1828.

FARMER, Ruth, w. Nathaniel, July 25, 1753.

FASSET (see Fassett), John, Dr., Jan. 30, 1736–7, in 67th y. [Fassett, G.R.]
Josiah, Capt., Feb. 18, 1740–1, in 54th y. [Fassett, C.R. G.R.]
Josiah, s. Josiah and Joanna, Jan. 27, 1753. [Jan. 28, C.R.]
Josiah, Capt., Aug. 20, 1766, in 52d y.
Josiah, s. Asa and Margaret, Aug. 20, 1779, a. 11 m. 24 d.
Mary, wid. Dr. John, Mar. 19, 1748–9. C.R.

FASSETT (see Fasset), Calley, d. Joseph and Dorothy, Aug. 22, 1775, a. 17. G.R.
Jonathan, s. Josiah, Sept. 30, 1730. C.R.
———, wid., paralytic disorder, Dec. 15, 1800, a. 82. C.R.
———, w. Asa of Alstead, jaundice, Oct. 21, 1804, a. 59. C.R.

FIELD, Peter W., colored, b. Northborough, s. Peter and Filena, strangulation, May 6, 1847, a. 6 y. 10 m.

FITCH, Abel, Oct. 16, 1839, a. 30. G.R.
Adelaide, d. Joel and Susannah, croup, Oct. 24, 1846, a. 6.

FITCH, Alford, s. Jeremiah and Lydia, Oct. 10, 1785.
Benjamin, July 7, 1770.
Daniel, s. Zachariah and w., consumption, Oct. 12, 1843, a. 80.
David, July 27, 1813, a. 70 y. 55 d. [a. 70, G.R.]
Ebenezer, s. Zech[a]r[iah] and Eliz[abet]h, Sept. 6, 1749. [s. Zachariah, Sept. 7, C.R.]
Elizabeth, d. Jeremiah and Elizabeth, Oct. 6, 1750.
Eliz[abeth], wid., old age, Sept. 12, 1803, a. "80 odd." C.R.
Elizabeth, Mar. 1, 1825, a. 73.
Elizebeth, w. Zachariah, Mar. 12, 1790.
Ellen, d. Albert and Almira, dysentery, Aug. 4, 1848, a. 1 y. 11 m.
Esther, d. Zech[a]r[iah] and Eliz[abet]h, Sept. —, 1749. [d. Zachariah, Sept. 23, C.R.]
Eunice, wid. Samuel, Aug. 27, 1767, a. 91.
Hannah, w. David Jr., Dec. 22, 1808, a. 26 y. 10 m. 16 d. [Dec. 22, 1805, G.R.]
Henry Brainerd, s. Abel and Nancy, July —, 1839, a. 3 m. G.R.
Isaac, s. Benjamin and Miriam, July 24, 1773, in 22d y. G.R.
Isaac, s. David, "suddenly with canker in his bowels," Feb. 5, 1797, a. 15. C.R. [s. David and Mary, Feb. 6, a. 15 y. 21 d, G.R.]
Isaac, s. David and Olive, Feb. 13, 1825, a. 1 m. 21 d. G.R.
Jeremiah, Dec. 29, 1808, a. 66 y. 3 m. 2 d.
Joel, m., s. Moses, fall from scaffold, Aug. 5, 1845, a. 51.
John, May 31, 1820, a. 81. G.R.
Jonathan Simonds, s. David and Olive, Jan. 25, 1819. [a. 4, G.R.]
Joseph, s. Joseph and Sarah, Sept. 21, 1736, in 3d y.
Joseph, Capt., Feb. 7, 1769, in 68th y.
Lucy, d. Zech[a]r[iah] and Eliz[abet]h, Sept. —, 1749. [d. Zachariah, Sept. 11, C.R.]
Lydia, ch. Benjamin and Miriam, Mar. 11, 1759, a. 14. G.R.
Lydia, d. Jeremiah Jr. and Lydia, Feb. 24, 1773.
Lydia, d. Jeremiah Jr. and Lydia, Aug. 12, 1778.
Lydia, b. Westford, wid. Joseph, lock jaw, Jan. 24, 1849, a. 51.
Marshal, s. Nathan and Loisa, abscess, Apr. 27, 1845, a, 4 m. 11 d.
Mary, w. David, Sept. 19, 1829, a. 82. G.R.
Mary Fowle, d. David Jr. and Olive, Aug. 4, 1806, a. 5 m. 23 d. [dysentery, a. 6 m., C.R.]
Matthew, Aug. 3, 1811, a. 66.
Moses, Capt., Aug. 1, 1821, a. 37.
Moses, Dea., Oct. 12, 1825, a. 71. [in 71st y., G.R.]
Nathan, s. Benja[min] and Miriam, May 13, 1755. [in 7th y., G.R.]

FITCH, Nathan, s. Moses and Rachel, Feb. 9, 1806.
Nathan, s. Capt. Joel and Susanna, Oct. 6, 1825.
Rachel, w. Dea. Moses, May 23, 1817, in 59th y. G.R.
Ruth, d. Joseph and Sarah, Oct. 2, 1749. [d. Lt. Joseph, Oct. 12, C.R.]
Sally, w. Alford, Aug. 23, 1820. [w. Olford, a. 23, G.R.]
Samuel, Apr. 4, 1742.
Sarah, w. Lt. Joseph, Jan. 22, 1749-50. [in 40th y., G.R.]
Susanna, d. Capt. Joel and Susanna, Jan. 17, 1824.
Susanna, d. Capt. Joel and Susanna, Aug. 14, 1825.
Zechariah, old age, Dec. 8, 1800, a. 88. C.R.
———, wid., "with the infirmities of age," Aug. 25, 1797, a. 84. C.R.
———, ch. Moses, canker rash, Mar. —, 1800, a. 2 y. 4 m. C.R.
———, ch. Lucy, complicated disorder, Apr. 4, 1802, a. 13 m. C.R.
———, w. David Jr., child bed fever, Dec. 22, 1803, a. 27. C.R.

FOSTER, Abner, s. Noah and Gracy, Mar. 6, 1828, a. 24. G.R.
Grace, w. Noah, consumption, Nov. 16, 1806, a. 29. C.R.

FRAZIER, Eliza, wid., b. Woburn, d. Joseph Webber and Ruth, typhus fever, Aug. 25, 1844, a. 40.

FREEMAN, Peter, colored, consumption, May 7, 1807, a. 57. C.R.

FRENCH, Joseph, Lt., h. Elizabeth, Nov. 26, 1732, in 83d y. [a. 83, G.R.]
Samuel, Jan. 18, 1737-8. [Jan. 28, 1738, a. abt. 52, G.R.]

FULLER, Elmira C., d. James Wilson and Dolly, June 23, 1841, a. 29 y. 9 m. 3 d.

GARDNER, Hannah, d. David Fitch and Olive, brain fever, Jan. 21, 1844, a. 40. [Hannah P., w. Dr. Bela, Jan. 20, G.R.]

GILSON, Sam[ue]l, "belonging to a nother Town," fever, Nov. 17, 1801, a. 22. C.R.

GLEASON, Abigail, w. Jonas, Sept. 21, 1815.
Alfred W., s. Lewis P. and w., Aug. 6, 1843, a. 1 y. 1 m.
Benjamin, Sept. 18, 1847, a. 70. G.R.
Caroline, d. Lewis P. and Sophronia, Jan. 6, 1827.
Caroline Maria [d. Lewis P. and Lucy], July 27, 1833.
Deborah, Aug. 23, 1839, a. 89 y. 10 m. 12 d.
Dorcas, d. Jonas and Ruth, June 16, 1787, a. 10 m. 3 d.

GLEASON, John Augustus [dup. John A.], father of Lewis P., June 11, 1842 [dup. a. 72].
Jonas, Feb. 8, 1815.
Lewis Putnam Jr. [s. Lewis P. and Lucy], July 30, 1838.
Lucy, w. Lewis P., fever, Oct. 30, 1846, a. 39.
Lucy C., d. Lewis P. and Lucy, Aug. 7, 1847, a. 11 m.
Rebecca W., w. Benjamin of Boston, d. William Maxwell, Dec. 10, 1846, a. 63. G.R.
Ruth, w. Jonas, Apr. 3, 1793. [a. 46 y. 9 m., G.R.]
Sophronia, w. Lewis P., Jan. 13, 1827.
———, wid., infirmities of age, Dec. 19, 1805, in 89th y. C.R.
———, d. ———, consumption, July —, 1846, a. 72.

GOODALE, Eame [? Ame], Aug. 11, 1806, a. 77. [wid., suddenly, C.R.]

GOODING, ———, fits, Oct. 11, 1802, a. 12 d. C.R.

GOODRIDGE, Hannah, w. Capt. William, Jan. 20, 1819, a. 58. [a. 57, G.R.]

GOODWAIN (see Goodwin), ———, still born, buried Feb. 24, 1808. C.R.

GOODWIN (see Goodwain), Adaline, w. Joseph, d. Jacob Gragg and Sally, child bed fever, June 30, 1844, a. 30.
T., Mrs., Sept. 2, 1842, a. 44.

GRAGG, Charles, s. Charles and Eliot, ———.
Jacob, inflamation of the stomach, Nov. 14, 1845, a. 79.
Mary Josephine [dup. Josephine] [d. Charles O. and Eliot] [dup. fever], June 24, 1842 [dup. a. 4].

GREEN, Abel, buried Mar. 21, 1846.

GRIMES, Elizabeth, d. Jonathan, June 23, 1750. C.R.
Mary, w. William, July 15, 1742.

GROVER, Thomas, s. Wid. Grover, Dec. 19, 1736. C.R.
Thomas, s. Thomas and Abigal, ———, in 11th y.

HADLEY, Simon, Sept. 30, 1801. ["dropped down instantly dead as he was walking thro' the room, supposed to have been occasioned by an appoplectic fit," a. 37, C.R.]

HALL, Ellen Josephine, b. Groton, d. Stephen and Harriet, consumption, June 14, 1849, a. 4 y. 5 w.

HALYETON [?], Sarah, w. Richard, "Late wife of Cap. Josiah Fasset," Jan. 30, 1754, in 66th y.

HAPGOOD, Henry Augustas, b. Concord, s. Cyrus and Ellen, scarlet fever, Mar. 4, 1849, a. 3 y. 9 m. 18 d.

HARTWEL (see Hartwell, Heartwel, Heartwell), Wiliam, s. Wiliam and Deborah, Apr. 13, 1736. [William Hartwell, s. William Jr., C.R.]

William, Dec. 11, 1742, in 72d y. [Heartwell, C.R.] [Hartwell, G.R.]

HARTWELL (see Hartwel, Heartwel, Heartwell), Abigal (Hartwel), w. Isac, May 30, 1733. [Abigail, w. Isaac, C.R.] [Abigail, in 38th y., G.R.]
Benjamin Franklin, s. Joseph and Hannah, cholera infantum, Sept. 25, 1848, a. 8 m.
Betsey, d. ——— Mead, consumption, Aug. 18, 1845, a. 78.
Desire, wid. Sam[ue]l, Aug. 30, 1824. [a. 68 y. 2 m., G.R.]
Elizabeth, wid. Joseph, Aug. 16, 1845, a. 78. G.R.
Jemima, w. Joseph, July 13, 1786, a. 56. G.R.
Joanna, w. William, Oct. 30, 1808, a. 39.
Joseph, s. Joseph and Jemima, Sept. 28, 1753. [Heartwell, C.R.] [a. 1 y. 4 m., G.R.]
Joseph, July 7, 1792, a. 69. G.R.
Joseph [h. Elizabeth], Aug. 3, 1840, a. 78. G.R.
Lydia, d. Joseph and Jemima, Feb. 13, 1788, a. 30. G.R.
Mary, wid. Timothy, Apr. 22, 1808, a. 89. [lung fever, C.R.]
Naomi S., w. Joseph 3d, May 5, 1840, a. 33. G.R.
Rebekah, w. Stephen, Aug. 13, 1790. [Heartwell, a. 79, G.R.]
Ruth, d. William and Deborah, Feb. 8, 1772.
Samuel, Apr. 2, 1823, a. 67.
Sarah Joanna, d. Amos and Louisa, Nov. 19, 1823.
Stephen July 12, 1792, a. 76. G.R.
Timothy, "with a complicated disorder," Dec. 27, 1797, a. 85. C.R.
William, May 8, 1819, in 49th y. G.R.
———, d. Timothy and Mary, Mar. 28, 1753. [Heartwell, inf. d. Timothy, C.R.]

HASTINGS, Jacob G., s. Justus P. and Maria L., cholera infantum, Aug. 9, 1844, a. 6 m. 18 d.
Jason, s. William, Oct. 8, 1749. C.R.

HAYNES, Nelson H., s. Stephen and Rachel, Feb. 25, 1847, a. 27. [Horatio Nelson, Feb. 23, G.R.]

HAYNES, Rachel, w. Stephen, disease of the liver [and] consumption, Sept. 19, 1847, a. 51 m. [*sic*, 51 y.] [a. 31, G.R.]

HAYWARD, John Augustus, s. John W. and Lydia H., Aug. 31, 1828.

Lucy, w. Mather, dropsey, Apr. 11, 1847, a. 70.

HEARTWEL (see Hartwel, Hartwell, Heartwell], Daniel, July 10, 1745. [Heartwell, C.R.]

Deborah, w. John, June 15, 1744. [Heartwell, June 14, C.R.] [Hartwell, June 14, in 68th y., G.R.]

HEARTWELL (see Hartwel, Hartwell, Heartwel), Deborah, w. William, Dec. 31, 1745. C.R.

John, Nov. 16, 1747. [Nov. 16, 1746, C.R.] [Nov. 16, 1746, in 74th y., G.R.]

Mary, w. Stephen, July 12, 1752.

Oliver, s. William, Dec. 14, 1745. C.R.

Ruth, wid. Will[ia]m, Feb. 17, 1751–2. C.R. [Hartwell, Feb. 7, in 77th y., G.R.]

Timothy, s. William, Sept. 21, 1745. C.R.

William, Apr. 20, 1746. C.R.

———, d. Timothy and Mary, June 5, 1750. [inf. d. Timothy, C.R.]

HILL, Lucy, d. Josiah and Susanna, July 30, 1801, a. 7 m. 19 d. [hooping cough, C.R.]

Lucy, d. Josiah and Susanna, Sept. 25, 1807. [lung fever, suddenly, a. 5, C.R.]

Mary, b. Chelmsford, d. Peter Proctor and Mary, neuralgia, Feb. 1, 1847, a. 68 y. 3 m. 16 d.

Susanna, w. Josiah, Feb. 15, 1818, a. 50 y. 3 m. 9 d.

HINDMAN, Caldwell F. of Boston, Nov. 22, 1835, a. 31. G.R.

HODGMAN, Mary, Mrs., consumption, Feb. —, 1843, a. 31.

HOLLIS, Lucy, w. Silas, consumption, May 6, 1847, a. 22 y. 10 m.

HOSMER, Ellen M., d. Benjamin G. and Olive, canker, Sept. 20, 1846, a. 2.

Ruth, b. Brantree, w. Castalio, dysentery, Aug. 13, 1849, a. 67 y. 7 m. 11 d.

Sarah, Mar. 18, 1820, a. 8 y. 3 m. G.R.

———, d. Castilio and Mary Jr., affection of the spine, Oct. 29, 1845, a. 3 m.

HUTCHINSON, Bartholonew, s. Benjamin and Sarah, Sept. 20, 1749. [Bartholemew, C.R.]
Benjamin [h. Sarah], Mar. 13, 1780, a. 80. G.R.
Benjamin, Mar. 5, 1815, a. 91. G.R.
John, s. Benjman and Sarah, Sept. 1, 1749. [s. Benjamin and Sarah, a. 13, G.R.]
John, s. Benj[amin] and Rebekah, Aug. 14, 1757.
Mary, d. Benjamin and Sarah, Sept. 14, 1749.
Rebecca, May 24, 1814, a. 91. G.R.
Sarah, w. Benjamin, Apr. 12, 1767, a. 66. G.R.
Selina Ann, d. Hezekiah and Rachel, Apr. 14, 1808. [fits, Apr. 12, a. 6 w., C.R.]
Susannah, d. Benjamin and Rebecca, June 4, 1815, a. 61. G.R.

IERLAND, Anna, w. Isaiah, d. Thomas Bacon, Oct. 3, 1770.

JACK, Allice, colored, "occasioned by falling into the fire in a fit," Oct. 12, 1804, a. "upwards of 30." C.R.

JAMES, ———, Mr., June 24, 1753, in 36th y.

JOHNSON, Ella, d. Obediah P., cholera infantum, Aug. 31, 1847, a. 9 m.
Samuel S., consumption, July 21, 1843, a. 1 y. 1 m.

JONES, Ebenezer, s. Ebenezer and Mary, Oct. 9, 1758.
Isaac, s. Col. Timothy and Rebekah, June 28, 1788. [s. Capt. Timothy and Rebekah, Jan. 27, a. 6 y. 1 m., G.R.]
John, s. Col. Timothy and Rebekah, Dec. 11, 1796, a. 23, "a then member of Cambridge Colledge." ["Dropsy, and other disorders," Dec. 10, C.R.]
John, s. Timothy and Susan, Aug. 22, 1817.
John Isaac, July 13, 1814, a. 18. G.R.
Rebecca, d. Timothy and Susan, July 3, 1820.
Rebekah, w. Timothy Esq., Aug. 13, 1807, a. 58. [Rebecca, wid., mortification, C.R.]
Susan, d. Timothy and Susan, Mar. 24, 1809.
Susan, w. Timothy, June 26, 1820. [Susanna P., a. 34, G.R.]
Tabitha, "a Girl who lived wth. Mr John Lane Junr," July 31, 1749. C.R.
Timothy, Esq., June 1, 1804, a. 55. [Col. Timothy, lung fever, C.R.]
Timothy, s. Timothy and Susan, Feb. 23, 1821. [s. Timothy and Susanna, a. 14, G.R.]

KENDAL, Jacob, s. Jacob and Alice, May 24, 1737, in 20th y.

KIDDER, Ben[j]amin, s. Benjamin and Hannah, Aug. 8, 1735.
Hannah, d. Benjamin, July 8, 1735. C.R.
Hannah, d. Benjamin and Hannah, Aug. 15, 1736.
Hannah, d. Benja[min] and Hannah, Oct. 24, 1740.
Hannah, w. Benjamin, July 5, 1752. [a. 48, G.R.]

LANE, Abigail, w. Capt. James, Feb. 25, 1773, in 77th y. [Abigail (Farmer), third w. Capt. James, a. 77, G.R.]
Abigail, w. Capt. James, "formerly the wife of M^r. John Meriam," Nov. 15, 1793, a. 83. [fourth w. Capt. James, "formerly the wife of Lieut. John Merriam," Nov. 5, G.R.]
Abigail F., d. Solomon and Sarah, July 17, 1800. [dysentery, July 18, a. 16 m., C.R.] [Abigail French, G.R.]
Abner, s. John, dysentery, Aug. 9, 1806, a. 20. C.R. [s. John and Ruhamah, Aug. 9, 1826, a. 21, G.R.]
Andrew, "Abcess within," May —, 1842, a. 22.
Andrew, s. Job and Mary, ——, 1842.
Anna, d. Lt. Job, Sept. 8, 1735. C.R.
Anna, b. Waltham, w. Eliab B., d. Jotham Welington and Priscilla, dysppsy, May 28, 1844, a. 67. [May 30, G.R.]
Benjamin, Mr., Jan. 25, 1754. C.R. [s. Dea. Job and Martha, in 25th y., G.R.]
Catherine W., w. Oliver W., July 30, 1841.
Catren, w. John, Apr. 1, 1731, in 40th y. [Katharine, C.R.] [Katherine, w. Col. John, G.R.]
Chary, w. Capt. James, Dec. 16, 1764. [Chary (Wellington), second w. Capt. James, a. 70, G.R.]
Daniel, s. Samuel and Hannah, Oct. 28, 1785.
Daniel, s. Solomon and Sarah, Oct. 3, 1803. [dysentery and canker in bowels, a. 3, C.R.]
David, A. M., s. James and Martha, Sept. 29, 1750, in 23d y., "deceased abroad." G.R.
David, s. Capt. James and Martha, Dec. 29, 1756.
David, Sept. 10, 1842, a. 83. G.R.
Enoch, s. Solomon and Sarah, Oct. 11, 1799. [nervous fever, a. 6 y. and abt. 8 m., C.R.]
Francis, s. John Jr. and Ruth, Feb. 23, 1749–50.
Galen, s. Eliab and Anna, Nov. 21, 1811, a. 7 m. G.R.
Gracy Foster, d. John and Ruhamah, Nov. 16, 1806, a. 30. G.R.
Hannah, d. Lt. Job and Martha, Dec. 27, 1733.
Hannah, d. Maj. John and Hannah, June 24, 1741.
Hannah, wid. Col. John, Apr. 22, 1769, in 74th y.
Hannah, w. Samuel, Sept. 29, 1796, a. 57 y. 20 d. [jaundice, C.R.]

LANE, Henry, s. Abner B. and Lydia, su[i]cidal hanging, Dec. 5, 1847, a. 16.
Henry Francis, s. Oliver W. and Catherine, May 1, 1841.
Isaac, s. James and Mary, May 24, 1803. [consumption, a. 37, C.R.] [Nov. 24, G.R.]
James, Capt., Apr. 11, 1783, a. 86 y. 8 m. [a. 87, G.R.]
James, Jan. 4, 1799. [sore in his throat, a. 73, C.R.]
James, Oct. 20, 1836, a. 83. G.R.
Job Sr., Sept. 9, 1744. C.R. [Sept. 19, a. 77, G.R.]
Job, Dea., Aug. 9, 1762, a. 73. G.R.
Job, Ens., s. Job and Susanna, Dec. 22, 1788, a. 32 y. 6 m. 9 d.
Job, June 11, 1796, a. 79. ["suddenly with cramp in his stomach," a. 78, C.R.]
Job, s. David and Molly, Nov. 15, 1814. [a. 26, G.R.]
John, Dec. 7, 1789, a. 69. G.R.
John, mortification, Feb. 22, 1808, a. 61. C.R. [a. 62, G.R.]
John, Col. [h. Hannah], ———. [Sept. 23, 1763, a. 72, G.R.]
Jonathan, Mar. 4, 1808, a. 44. [consumption, C.R.]
Jonathan Abbott, s. Jonathan and Ruhamah, ——— [rec. after Oct. 23, 1818]. [Aug. 24, 1820, G.R.]
Josiah, s. John and Sarah, Mar. 15, 1762. [Mar. 5, G.R.]
Josiah [s. Ziba and Hannah], Nov. 5, 1780.
Josiah, s. Solomon and Sarah, Apr. 18, 1787. [Apr. 8, G.R.]
Josiah Stearns, s. Josiah and Amelia, Sept. 22, 1815. [Josiah S., only ch. Josiah and Amitia, a. 21 m., G.R.]
Laura Ann [d. Oliver W. and Catherine], Apr. 26, 1834.
Love, d. James and Martha, Aug. 13, 1735. [d. Ens. James, Aug. 3, C.R.]
Luke, fever, Aug. 27, 1801, a. 33. C.R. G.R.
Lydia, d. Timothy and Lydia, Oct. 23, 1765.
Lydia, d. Timothy and Lydia, July 13, 1796, a. 24 y. 5 m. 27 d. [consumption, C.R.]
Lydia, wid., bilious fever, Aug. 4, 1801, a. 72. C.R. [wid. Timothy, Aug. 31, G.R.]
Martha, w. Dea. Job, Sept. 14, 1740. C.R. [a. 49, G.R.]
Martha, w. Capt. James, July 3, 1762. [first w. Capt. James, a. 64, G.R.]
Mary, d. James and Martha, Mar. 4, 1736–7. [Mercy, d. Ens. James, C.R.]
Mary, w. Job, Sept. 7, 1746. [wid. Job, C.R.] [a. 65, G.R.]
Mary, wid. Dea. Job, Dec. 11, 1783.
Mathew, s. Maj. John [and] Katharine, Aug. 5, 1741. [Matthew, C.R.]
Molly, w. David, Dec. 12, 1820, a. 50 y. 6 m. G.R.

LANE, Molly, w. James, old age, Feb. 16, 1848, a. 96. [wid. James, a. 96 y. 8 m., G.R.]
Nathan, s. Timothy and Lydia, Dec. 1, 1794, in 27th y.
Phebe, w. David, July 8, 1838, a. 65. G.R.
Rebekah, d. Samuel, Nov. 27, 1791.
Roger, first s. John and Ruhamah, Nov. 16, 1794, a. 16 m. G.R.
Ruhamah, d. Jonathan and Ruhamah ——— [rec. after May 6, 1816]. [Apr. 10, 1817, G.R.]
Ruhamah, w. John, Apr. 30, 1817, a. 63. G.R.
Ruth, w. John Jr., Aug. 13, 1759, in 36th y. [Ruth (Bowman), G.R.]
Ruth, w. Samuel, d. Stephen Davis and Elizabeth, Oct. 21, 1772, in 33d y.
Samuel, s. Capt. John and Catern, Apr. 1, 1734, in 7th y.
Samuel, s. Job and Mary, Nov. 25, 1736, in 21st y. [s. Job Sr., C.R.] [a. 21, G.R.]
Samuel, Jan. 26, 1780, a. 65. G.R.
Sam[ue]l, bileous colic, June 26, 1802, a. 65. C.R.
Sarah, d. Lt. Job and Martha, Oct. 7, 1733. [Oct. 4, C.R.]
Sarah, w. Solomon, Aug. 13, 1825. [a. 69, G.R.]
Solomon, Mar. 23, 1812, a. 56. G.R.
Solomon, Feb. 1, 1837, a. 80. G.R.
Stephen, s. Ens. James, July 4, 1740. C.R.
Susanna, d. Capt. James and Martha, Feb. 24, 1749–50.
Susanna, w. Job, Mar. 24, 1775.
Timothy, Dec. 3, 1793, in 72d y. [a. 72, G.R.]
Whippel, ch. Lt. Job and Martha, Oct. 4, 1728.
William, s. Job and Mary, ———.
———, ch. Jona[than], canker rash, Jan. 9, 1800, a 5 y. 9 m. C.R. [Rollin, s. Jonathan and Hannah, a. 4, G.R.]
———, ch. Jona[than], canker rash, Jan. 15, 1800, a. 7 m. C.R. [Elizabeth, d. Jonathan and Hannah, G.R.]
———, ch. Jona[than], suddenly, May 20, 1801, a. 6 m. C.R. [Myra, d. Jonathan and Hannah, May 2, a. 5 m., G.R.]
———, ch. Fanny, "suddenly. Canker in the bow[els]," June 26, 1801, a. 8 m. C.R.
———, w. Samuel, complicated complaint, Sept. 19, 1807, a. 69. C.R.
———, "Mrs. Josiah," Sept. 21, 1815, a. 28. [Mr. Josiah S., G.R.]

LAWRENCE, Mary, w. Jonathan, cancer, Dec. 3, 1846, a. 69.

LEMMON, Philip, drowned in Concord River, Apr. 16, 1746. C.R.

LOCKE, Esther, b. Lexington, w. Ward, dysentery, Oct. 29, 1848, a. 47.

MALLET, Abigail, lung fever, Jan. 31, 1803, a. 75. c.r.

MARCUM [?], Isaac of Middleton, Conn., a violent fever, Aug. 22, 1801, a. 22. c.r.

MAXWELL, Hugh, Mar. 19, 1759, a. 59. g.r.
Rhoda, Dec. 8, 1875. g.r.
Sarah, w. William, Apr. 21, 1833, a. 76. g.r.
William, May 10, 1832, a. 79. g.r.
———, ch. W[illia]m, dysentery, Aug. 27, 1801, a. 3. c.r.

McCORDEY, ———, s. Thomas, Apr. 13, 1749. c.r.

MEAD, Anna, Jan. 19, 1818, a. 49.
Asa Jr., s. Asa and Abigail, consumption, Aug. 10, 1848, a. 44.
Desire, w. Stephen, Sept. 9, 1797, a 59 y. 6 m. 15 d. [Meads, jaundice, c.r.] [Desire (Bachelder), "former wife of Mr. Joseph Brown," g.r.]
Esther, d. Jonathan and Keziah, old age, Nov. 9, 1848, a. 73.
John, s. Stephen and Desire, June 12, 1799, a. 22. [canker rash, c.r.] [Jan. 12, g.r.]
Jonathan, consumption, June 4, 1847, a. 73.
Stephen, Jan. 30, 1808, a. 71. [apoplexy, c.r.]

MELVIN, Hannah of Carlisle, paralytic, Apr. —, 1799. c.r.

MERIAM (see Merriam, Merriams), Abigail, d. John Esq. and Abigail, Aug. 16, 1749. [Merriam, d. Ens. John (Meriam), c.r.]
Elizabeth, w. Ebenezer of Concord, "formerly wife to Mr. Stephen Davis," June 5, 1752, a. 64 y. 2 m. 3 d.
John, Sept. 20, 1767. [Lt. John Merriam, a. 67, g.r.]
John, Lt., Dec. 26, 1794, in 60th y.
Josephus, s. William and Esther, Aug. 25, 1783.
Louisa How, July 2, 1799, a. 6 y. 9 m. [Luisa How Merriam, canker rash, c.r.]
Mary, w. Dea. Nath[ani]ll, May 19, 1764.
Nathanael, s. John and Abigail, Sept. 15, 1758, "In His Majestys' Service at Lake George."
Nathaniel, s. Samuel (Merriam) and Allise, ———.
Nathanill, Dea., Dec., 11, 1738. [Dea. Nathanael, suddenly, c.r.] [Dea. Nathaniel Merriam, a. 66, g.r.]
Rebekah, d. John and Hannah, Oct. 10, 1765.
Rebekah, d. John and Hannah, Mar. 2, 1790, in 24th y.

MERIAM, Samuel, Mar. 22, 1761.
Sarah, w. Samuel, Dec. 1, 1743. C.R.
Thaddeus, s. Lt. John and Abigail, Oct. 24, 1754.
William, s. John Esq. and Abigal, Aug. 15, 1749. [s. Ens. John, C.R.]
William Bellamy, s. William and Esther, Sept. 7, 1778, a. 2 y. 1 m. 1 d.

MERRIAM (see Meriam, Merriams), Esther, w. William (Meriam), child bed, Mar. 17, 1785, a. 33 y. 9 m. 8 d. [w. Lt. William, G.R.]
John 2d, s. John A. and Nanecy, poisoned by tobacco, Jan. 11, 1846, a. 2 y. 7 m.
Mary Addeline, d. John and Mary, Apr. 28, 1807. [lung fever, a. 14 m., C.R.]
Nathaniel, Mr., May 9, 1802. [infirmities of age, a. 82, C.R.]
Olive, w. Nathaniel, Nov. 25, 1806. [wid., paralytic stroke, Nov. 24, a. 79, C.R.]

MERRIAMS (see Meriam, Merriam), ———, ch. Sam[ue]l, "suddenly with canker in his bowels," Feb. 8, 1797, a. 19 m. C.R.

MERRITT, George, s. Edward and Betsey, typhus fever, ———, 1847 [rec. after Dec. 5].

MONROE (see Munroe), Sally, d. James Wright and Dorcas, consumption, Mar. 5, 1844, a. 35.
Sophronia A., d. Abel and Sally, fever, Apr. 27, 1844, a. 2 y. 6 m.

MOOR (see Moore, More, Morr), Mary, "formerly wife M^r. James Lane," Apr. 2, 1806. [More, w. Capt. John, "complaint on her liver," Apr. 3, a. 73, C.R.] [Moore, second w. Capt. John, Apr. 2, a. 76, G.R.]

MOORE (see Moor, More, Morr), Elizabeth, d. John, Aug. 31, 1743. C.R.
Elizabeth, w. John, Feb. 2, 1744–5. [Elizabeth (Wheeler), second w. John, G.R.]
John, Aug. 21, 1765, a. 58. G.R.
John, Capt., infirmities of age, Sept. 24, 1807, a. 78. C.R. [s. John, Sept. 27, G.R.]
John, cancer, Oct. 8, 1847, a. 60.
Richard, s. John, Nov. 16, 1744. C.R.

MORE (see Moor, Moore, Morr), Joseph, "with a paralytic ended in a mortification," Mar. 18, 1802, a. 70. C.R.

MORE, ———, w. Capt. John, paralytic disorder, July 5, 1798, a. 70. C.R. [Mary, first w. Capt. John, July 6, 1797, a. 73, G.R.]

MORR (see Moor, Moore, More), Elizabeth, w. John, Mar. 28, 1732. [Moor, C.R.] [Moore, Mar. 18, a. 25, G.R.]

MUNROE (see Monroe), ———, d. Josiah and Susanna, Jan. 5, 1769.

NEWTON, Amittai [w. Simon], Aug. 28, 1756, in 25th y. [Neuton, Aug. 29, a. 25, G.R.]

NICHOLS, Sally Miranda, w. Stephen, consumption, June 6, 1848, a. 40.

PAGE (see Paige), Amity, w. John, Dec. 25, 1771.
Anna, wid. Thomas, July 10, 1810, a. 73. G.R.
Benjamin, s. Nathaniel and Lydia, disease of the liver, Jan. 13, 1848, a. 34.
Betsey B., consumption, June 25, 1842, a. 28. [w. Silas W., a. 37, G.R.]
Christopher, Nov. 11, 1786, in 79 thy. [s. Nathaniel 2d, a. 80, G.R.]
David, Jan. 11, 1819.
Dolley, b. Lexington, d. Ebenezer and Dorothy, Apr. 23, 1772.
Dolly Eveline, d. Joshua and Elsey, Nov. 29, 1818.
Dorithy, w. Ebenezer, Feb. 6, 1779, a. 41 y. 7 m. 4 d. [Dorothy, G.R.]
Ebenezer, June 9, 1784, a. 47 y. 6 d.
Hannah, b. Woburn, w. Moses, consumption, Aug. 8, 1849, a. 64 y. 18 w.
Isaac F., s. Nath[anie]l and Lydia, phthysic, Nov. 21, 1844, a. 39 y. 2 m. 20 d., in Lexington.
Isanna Harrington, d. Larkin P. and Rebecca, dysentery, Aug. 1, 1848, a. 4.
John, Feb. 18, 1782. [Cornet John, a. 78, G.R.]
John, Capt., June 29, 1848, a. 81. G.R.
John H., ch. Silas W. and Betsey B., Feb. 27, 1841, a. 18 m. G.R.
Joshua, consumption, Nov. 27, 1842, a. 64.
Lucy, d. Ebenezer and Dorothy, Aug. 14, 1775.
Lucy, b. Burlington, w. William, Dec. 18, 1849, a. 62.
Lydia, w. Capt. Christopher, Feb. 20, 1808, a. 64. G.R.
Mary, w. Benjamin of Quinsy, "a dropsical and consumptive case," funeral July 26, 1805. C.R.

PAGE, Moses, s. Ebenezer and Dorithy, Aug. 9, 1775.
Nathaniel, Cornet, Apr. 6, 1779, a. 76. G.R.
Nathaniel, s. Nathaniel Jr. and Lydia, Apr. 10, 1808. [fever, a. 11 m., C.R.] [s. Nathaniel Jr. and Lucy, G.R.]
Nathaniel, Mr., July —, 1819. [July 31, a. 77, G.R.]
Pattey, w. William, Apr. 14, 1809, a. 69. G.R.
Rachel, wid. John, "late wid. Capt. Joseph Fitch," Jan. 26, 1801, a. 89. ["with infirmities of age," C.R.]
Sally, w. Joshua, Nov. 25, 1814.
Samuel, Jan. 31, 1839, a. 22, in New Loudon, N.H. ["member of the junior class of Dartmouth College, N.H." G.R.]
Samuel, consumption, Dec. 10, 1843, a. 32.
Sarah, w. Nathaniel, Aug. 2, 1839, a. 92. [Aug. 22, 1834, G.R.]
Sarah Eveline, d. Joshua and Sally, Feb. 24, 1810.
Susanna, d. Nathaniel and Hannah, Jan. 26, 1772, a. 75.
Susanna, wid. Christopher, July 20, 1792, in 83d y.
Susanna, ch. Silas W. and Betsey B., May 4, 1841, a. 4 y. 6 m. G.R.
William, Feb. 10, 1812, a. 74. G.R.
William Edward, s. Larkin P. and Rebecca, dysentery, Aug. 12, 1848, a. 1 y. 5 m. 20 d.
———, ch. Joshua, still born, funeral July 23, 1805. C.R.
———, w. Capt. Christopher, dropsy, Feb. 20, 1808, a. 64. C.R.

PAIGE (see Page), Job, s. Christopher, Apr. 7, 1754. C.R. [Page, ch. Christopher and Susanna, a. 5 y. 10 m. 7 d., G.R.]
Lucy, d. Christopher and Susanna, Mar. 26, 1754. [Page, a. 2, G.R.]
Mary, d. John and Rebakan, Oct. 13, 1745. [d. "Cor^t." John, C.R.]
Mary, d. John and Rebekah, Oct. 21, 1753. [d. "Cor^t." John, Oct. 23, C.R.]
Nathanael, s. "Cor." Nathanael Jr., Mar. 26, 1750–1. [Nathaniel *tertius*, C.R.]
Nathaniel, "Cor.," Mar. 2, 1755, a. 75. [Nathanael, C.R.] [Cornet Nathaniel Page, a. 76, G.R.]
Rebekah, w. "G^r." John, July 12, 1755, a. 43.
Susanna, w. "Cor^t." Nathanael Sr., Sept. 2, 1746. C.R. [Page, d. Col. John Lane 2d, a. 63, G.R.]
Susanna, d. Christopher and Susana, Sept. 8, 1746.
Susanna, d. Christopher and Susanna, Mar. 28, 1754. [Page, a. 3 y. 2 m. 20 d., G.R.]
Sussanna, d. "Co^r." John and Rebekah, Feb. 26, 1749–50. [Susanna, d. Cor^t." John, C.R.]
Thomas, July 31, 1809. [Page, a. 76, G.R.]

PARKER, Samuel, Aug. 9, 1741. C.R.
Sarah, wid., "formerly the wife of Mr. John Lane," Mar. 5, 1814, a. 88. G.R.

PARKHURST, Rhoda, w. Joseph, Sept. 28, 1815.

PEARCE (see Pierce).

PENNAMAN (see Penniman), Hannah, d. Rev. Joseph and Hannah, Dec. 22, 1790.

PENNIMAN (see Pennaman), Molly, d. Rev. J. [and Hannah], Aug. 21, 1778.

PERRY, John, s. Thomas, Feb. 28, 1753. C.R.
Thomas, s. Thomas, Jan. 25, 1754. C.R.

PHELPS, Joseph Thomas, s. Joseph and Drucilla, cholera infantum, Sept. 17, 1849, a. 10 m. 3 d.
Lorenzo Fremont, s. Lorenzo and Susannah, consumption, Oct. 23, 1849, a. 1 y. 10 m.
Susannah H., w. Lorenzo, consumption, Jan. 25, 1849, a. 24.

PIERCE, Augustus, ch. George, consumption, May 6, 1846, a. 33. [a. 30, G.R.]
George N., Mar. 24, 1848, a. 31. G.R.
———, s. Augustus, canker rash, May —, 1842, a. 3.

PIKE, ———, throat distemper, Aug. 24, 1801, a. 10. C.R.

PIPER, Alonzo, s. Daniel B. and Elizabeth, "desiase of the brain," Jan. 28, 1846, a. 4.
Alonzo, s. Daniel and Elizabeth, lung fever, June 26, 1847, a. 3 m.
Daniel Jr., s. Daniel B. and Elizabeth, cholera infantum, Oct. 7, 1848, a. 4 m.

POLLARD, Hannah, w. Oliver, June 9, 1752.
Hannah, consumption, July 30, 1842, a. 59.
Matthew, Nov. 15, 1801, a. 52. [consumption, C.R.]
Obed, widr., dropsey, Mar. 11, 1846, a. 62, in Lexington.
Oliver, July 11, 1788.
Oliver, May 28, 1831, a. 94. G.R.
Sarah, w. Jonathan, Dec. 16, 1762.
Susanna, July 9, 1786.
———, s. Jonathan and Sarah, Dec. 13, 1762.
———, w. Oliver, Feb. 20, 1840, a. 91 y. 4 m. G.R.

PORTER, Asa, ———, 1826.

PORTER, Bethiah, wid., Apr. 16, 1808, a. 85, "at her daughters in Lincoln." C.R.
Joseph, July 13, 1770, a. 52 y. 1 m. 3 d.
Joseph, s. William and Lucy, June 14, 1811, a. 21. G.R.
———, ch. W[illia]m, lung fever, Jan. 17, 1801, a. 1 m. C.R.
———, ch. W[illia]m, lung fever, Mar. 25, 1804, a. 9 w. C.R.

POWERS, Jonathan, s. Walter and Sarah, Jan. 14, 1754, in 19th y.
Sarah, w. Walter, May 10, 1739. C.R.

PRATT, Eliza Jane, b. Dunstable, d. Stephen and Rebecca, consumption, Sept. 6, 1848, a. 25.

PRESTON, Hannah, w. Dr. Amariah, Feb. 8, 1795. [in 26th y., G.R.]
Hannah, d. Dr. Amariah, Aug. 8, 1810, a. 15. G.R.
———, ch. Dr. Preston, dysentery, Sept. 7, 1800, a. 2 m. C.R.

PROCTOR, Susan, d. W[illia]m and Susan, June 2, 1843, a. 6 m.
William Jr., s. W[illia]m and w., fever, Nov. 21, 1843, a. 12.

PULSIFER, Betsey, w. Robert S., Sept. 29, 1822, a. 29.
Joseph of Boston, June 3, 1815, a. 25. G.R.

PUTNAM, Benjamin, Sept. 15, 1763, a. 38.
David, s. Cornelius of Sutton, Aug. 3, 1741. C.R.
Eunice, w. Benjamin, Oct. 5, 1762.
Israel, Dea., Nov. 12, 1760, in 62d y. [a. 62, G.R.]
Jonas, Mar. 10, 1818, a. 32.

QUIMBY, Rebecca, w. Dyer, July 7, 1820. [Rebeccah, July 8, a. 25 y. 5 m., G.R.]

RANDALL, Sarah, Mrs., Mar. 2, 1821, a. 44. G.R.

REED, Abigail, w. Capt. David, Sept. —, 1803, a. 44. ["suddenly, with a swelling in her arm, which began in one finger & gradually extended to the seat of life," Sept. 1, a. 43, C.R.] [Sept. 1, G.R.]
Addeline, Mar. 20, 1835, a. 10 m.
Amanda, Sept. 15, 1846, a. 26. G.R.
Anna, d. John and Hannah, Dec. 18, 1807, a. 20 y. 4 m. 16 d. [consumption, Nov. 18, a. 20, C.R.]
Augusta T., w. Ephriam, consumption, Nov. 27, 1845, a. 30.
Betsey, w. Oliver Jr., Oct. 22, 1802, a. 45. G.R.
Betsey, d. Reuben and Mary, May 3, 1808.
Betsey, d. Reuben and Mary, May 3, 1813, a. 3 y. 8 m. G.R.

REED, David, Capt. [h. Martha], Jan. 6, 1832.
Eliot, d. John and Ruhamah [(Brown) G.R.], Aug. 24, 1780, in 16th y.
Ephriam, consumption, Jan. 20, 1847, a. 30.
Grace, d. John and Ruhamah, Sept. 16, 1778, in 19th y. [Grace Page, G.R.]
Hannah, w. Lt. David, Apr. 29, 1790, a. 38 y. 8 m. 10 d. [w. Capt. David, a. 39, G.R.]
Harriet Ann, d. Sam[ue]l and Harriet, Jan. 2, 1837, a. 1 m.
Harriet Jane, Mar. 11, 1835, a. 4.
John Esq., Nov. 20, 1805, a. 74. [fever, a. 75, C.R.] [a. 75, G.R.]
John, s. John and Hannah, May 13, 1819.
John, s. David and Hannah, fever, Nov. 3, 1846, a. 75.
Lot, h. Lusibia, Sept. 24, 1821.
Malvina, d. Jesse and Ruth, dropsey, July 18, 1844, a. 21.
Martha, w. Capt. David, Jan. 31, 1834.
Martha S., w. Nathan O., Mar. 22, 1841, a. 24. G.R.
Mary, second w. Oliver, May 31, 1812, a. 32. G.R.
Mary Caroline, Mar. 12, 1835, a. 7.
Melissa, d. W[illia]m N., croup, Aug. 12, 1845, a. 1 y. 10 m.
Oliver, Sept. 18, 1811, in 83d y. G.R.
Oliver, Aug. 15, 1837, a. 81. G.R.
Reuben, Feb. 1, 1815, a. 56.
Roger, s. John and Ruhamah, old age, June 6, 1844, a. 81 y. 11 m. 22 d. [June 8, a. 82, G.R.]
Ruhamah, w. John Esq., June 9, 1798. ["with dropsy supposed to be upon her lungs," a. 67, C.R.] [Ruhamah (Brown), Jan. 9, G.R.]
Sally, "a nervous case," funeral Aug. 28, 1805, a. 40. C.R.
Sally, wid. Roger, old age, Feb. 8, 1849, a. 83.
Sally, b. Groton, wid. John, consumption, Aug. 15, 1849, a. 75.
Sarah, d. Benjamin and Sally, consumption, Oct. 7, 1846, a. 13.
Sarah, w. Roger, Feb. 8, 1849, a. 83. G.R.
———, d. David and Hannah, Mar. 22, 1790.
———, w. Oliver Jr., bileous colic, Oct. 22, 1802, a. " 40 odd." C.R.
———, ch. Ephraim, Sept. —, 1842.

RICE, Abi, w. David, Oct. 30, 1820, a. 31. G.R.
David, m., consumption, Jan. 19, 1849, a. 67.
———, w. David, ——— [rec. after Jan. 13, 1813].

RICHARDSON, Ruth, pleuricy, Apr. 19, 1842, a. 71.

ROBARTSON, Mary, d. John and Mary, Aug. 16, 1745.

ROBINSON, Elizabeth, paralytic, Dec. 1803, a. 57. C.R.
Jessie, consumption, Dec. 3, 1843, a. 76. [Dec. 1, 1842, C.R.]
Martha, Aug. 7, 1840, a. 21. C.R.
Mary, d. John, Aug. 12, 1745. C.R.
Mary, June 9, 1833, a. 20. C.R.

ROLE (see Rolfe), Daniel, Oct. 27, 1748, " Reputed to be in his Hundreth year." [Rolfe, C.R.]

ROLFE (see Rolf), Mary, w. Daniel, Mar. 5, 1737–8. C.R.

ROSS, ———, ch. John, worm fever, Oct. 13, 1798, a. 15 m. C.R.

RUSSELL, Hannah, w. Jabez, May 15, 1776.
Roxy B., b. Townsend, w. Royall, consumption, May 30, 1849 a. 50.
Royal, widr., b. Carlisle, " Caused by a fall," Oct. 7, 1849, a. 54.
———, s. Jabez and Hannah, July 9, 1752. [inf. s. Jabez, C.R.]

SAGE, Samuel, s. Sam[ue]l and Lucy, ——— [rec. after Apr. 8, 1818].

SHED, Sophia, w. Abel, Feb. 20, 1824, a. 41. G.R.

SHERMAN, Thaddeus, s. Rev. Nathaniel and Lydia, Aug. 22, 1765.

SIKES, Caroline Holmes, d. Oren and Julia K., Sept. 9, 1846, a. 2 y. 10 m.

SIMONDS, Anna, w. John, Aug. 23, 1826.
Eliza Ann, d. John and Anna, Sept. 16, 1826.
Harriet, consumption, Feb. 28, 1843, a. 24.
William, Mr., Sept. 13, 1755. C.R.
William, d. Zebedee and Amittai, June 8, 1838.
Zebedee, Dea., Sept. 20, 1826, a. 40.
Zebedee, s. Dea. Zebedee and Ammitai, May 29, 1827.

SKELTON, Edwin, s. Elijah and Sarah, bilious colic, Apr. 11, 1849, a. 28.
Emily, d. Elijah and Sarah, Sept. 7, 1822.
Lendel, s. Daze and Keziah, Aug. 30, 1796. [Skilton, worms, a. 11 m., C.R.]
Louisa, w. Elias, July 2, 1836, a. 24 y. 6 m.
Samuel, s. Elias and Louisa, Oct. 18, 1832. [a. 4 m., G.R.]

SLOAN, Dolley E., d. James Wilson and Dolly, Aug. 23, 1842, a. 33 y. 7 m. 27 d.

SLOAN, Eliza, consumption, Aug. 16, 1842, a. 34.
George W., June 5, 1841, a. 33 y. 6 m. 8 d.

SPALDING, Augustus, s. Charles and Elizabeth, July 31, 1834.
George, s. Charles and Elizabeth, July 13, 1832.

SPRAGUE, John (Sprage), s. John and Phebe, May 25, 1805,
    a. 16. [bilious and nervous fever, May 23, C.R.] [May 21,
    a. 16 y. 6 m., G.R.]
John, Mar. 4, 1810, a. 51.
Mary, d. John and Betsey, fever, Nov. 24, 1846, a. 51.
Sally, d. John and Phebe, Apr. 22, 1805, a. 18. [Sprage, suddenly with bilious fever, Apr. 26, C.R.] [Apr. 25, G.R.]

STEAPLES, Mary, "late wife of M.ʳ Daniel Davis," Feb. 2,
    1769, a. 87.

STEARNS (see Sterns), Abigail French, d. Rev. Samuel and
    Abigail, Nov. 2, 1798. [only ch. Samuel, dysentery, a. 11 w.,
    in Andover, C.R.]
Betsey, Mrs., dysentery, Sept. 17, 1842, a. 70. [w. Noah, a. 71,
    G.R.]
Betsey D., wid., d. Thaddeus Doirs and Sarah, scrofula, July 27,
    1844, a. 60 y. 6 m. 28 d. [a. 61, G.R.]
Edward, s. Edward and Lucy, May 24, 1768. [in 8th y. G.R.]
Edward, Capt., June 11, 1793, in 67th y. [a. 68, G.R.]
Edward, Lt., nervous fever, May 17, 1798, a. 30. C.R. [May
    18, G.R.]
Edward, s. Elijah and Elizabeth, Dec. 15, 1804. [Dec. 16, a.
    3 d., C.R.]
Edward Josiah, s. Elijah and Elizabeth, Dec. 16, 1806. [hectical complaint, a. 10 m., C.R.]
Elizabeth, w. Samuel, Mar. 12, 1749-50.
George Washington, s. Rev. Samuel and Abigail, Oct. 28, 1812.
Horatio Davis, s. William and Betsey, Dec. 28, 1803.
Lucy, d. Edward and Lucy, May 20, 1768. [in 13th y. G.R.]
Lucy, wid. Capt. Stearns, Nov. 28, 1802, in 70th y. [nervous
    fever, a. 68, C.R.]
Mary Elizabeth, d. Elijah Esq. and Elizabeth, July 12, 1818, a. 11.
    G.R.
Matilda Caroline, d. W[illia]m and Betsey, Jan. 4, 1808. [ch.
    William of Harvard, lung fever, a. 20 m., C.R.]
Polley, w. Edward, d. Col. Timothy Jones and Rebekah, June
    28, 1796, a. 27. [w. Lt. Edward, consumption, C.R.]
Sam[ue]l, Rev., Dec. 26, 1834. [in 65ᵗʰ y. and "39th of his ministry," G.R.]

STEARNS, Sarah, wid. Rev. Josiah of Epping, N.H., infirmities of age, Apr. 2, 1808, a. 76. C.R.
Simeon, consumption, Apr. 18, 1846, a. 74.
Solomon, s. Edward and Lucy, May 18, 1775. [s. Capt. Edward and Lucy, a. 19, G.R.]
William [h. Betsey], Sept. 9 [? 19], 1823, in " Batton rogue."

STERNS (see Stearns), John, father of Zachri, Elezar and Benjam[in], June 14, 1734, in 59th y. [Stearns, C.R.]

STRATTON, Sarah, d. Benj[ami]n, Jan. 14, 1754. C.R.

SWAIN, Hannah, w. Warren, Apr. 16, 1823, a. 27.
Hannah Malvina, d. Warren and Hannah, Mar. 24, 1823.

TAYLER (see Taylor), Hannah, w. David, Sept. 5, 1744. [Taylor, C.R.]

TAYLOR (see Tayler), Eunice, wid., May 7, 1737, a. 80. C.R. [w. John, a. 81, G.R.]
Lucey, d. David, Oct. 9, 1749. C.R.
Nathan, s. David, Oct. 9, 1747. C.R.

TENNY, John Y., consumption, Apr. —, 1842, a. 48.

THOMAS, Elizabeth, Apr. 6, 1839, a. 72. G.R.

THOMPSON, James, b. Ireland, "he said he had lived at Middleton in Connicticut was a Soldier in the Continental Army 4 or five Years. fell sick as he was traveling the Road at the house of Thaddeus Fitch the 17 day of April 1790 he Saith that he had two children at middleton in connicticut," Apr. 25, 1790, a. abt. 37.

THURSTON, Lucinda, d. Stephen and Philomela, Mar. 21, 1805. [consumption, Mar. 23, a. 8 m., C.R.]

WEBBER (see Weber), Artemas, s. Job and Sally, consumption, Dec. 19, 1846, a. 46.
Benjamin A., s. William and Betsey, mortification of typhoid fever, Aug. 9, 1846, a. 44.
Eliza F., Jan. 21, 1839, a. 33. G.R.
Fidelia, w. Hiram, Apr. 5, 1834. G.R.
Hannah, w. James, Jan. 20, 1835, a. 63. G.R.
Hannah R., d. James and Hannah, typhus fever, Sept. 11, 1844, a. 33 y. 11 m. 25 d. [Sept. 18, a. 34, G.R.]
Job, Oct. 10, 1838, a 69. G.R.
John, Capt., Apr. 29, 1808, a. 75.

WEBBER, John, s. John and Sally, influenza, Dec. 11, 1846, a. 86.
Joseph, m., s. John and Sarah, apoplexy, Aug. 24, 1844, a. 79 y. 10 m. 3 d.
Joseph T., s. Joseph and Eliza, May 29, 1844, a. 15, in Concord. [Joseph Thompson, June 1, a. 15 y. 9 m., G.R.]
Lydia, d. Asa and Eliot, Aug. 20, 1811.
Mary, w. William, May 24, 1817, a. 49. [Mary (Abbott), Mar. 24, G.R.]
Moses, s. William and Mary, July 28, 1811.
Polley, d. William and Mary, Sept. 13, 1793, a. 1 y. 3 m. 19 d.
Sarah, w. John, May 9, 1782, a. 38 y. 3 m. 9 d. [w. Capt. John, G.R.]
Susana, d. John and Sarah, June 28, 1774, a. 5 m.
Susannah (Page), second w. Capt. John, Feb. 5, 1825, a. 75. G.R.
Thomas, consumption, Aug. 8, 1846, a. 69.
William, Sept. 25, 1833, a. 71. G.R.
———, ch. James, Nov. 23, 1806, a. abt. 9 min. C.R.

WEBER (see Webber), Susanna, d. Benjamin and Susanna of Medford, Apr. 2, 1743. [Webber, d. Mrs. Paige, C.R.]

WELLINGTON (see Willington), Oliver, s. Benjamin and Mary, Aug. 31, 1749, in 15th y.

WELSH, John, "a Lad lived with Mr. James Miller," Nov. 28, 1736. C.R.

WHEELER (see Whelor), Anna, wid., "mortification occasioned by a small bruise on her arm," Mar. 14, 1804, a. 91. C.R.
Eunice, w. Richard, July 17, 1760.
Jacob S., s. Jacob and Mary A., consumption, Sept. 26, 1844, a. 4.
Mary A., b. Charlestown, w. Jacob, d. Caleb Hovey and Ann, consumption, July 29, 1844, a. 35.
———, s. Jacob and w., consumption, Nov. 6, 1843, a. 1.
———, w. Abner, consumption, Aug. 7, 1847, a. 44.
———, b. Charlestown, w. Jacob, consumption, Oct. 24, 1848, a. 34.

WHELOR (see Wheeler), Jemima, w. Richard, Sept. 9, 1743. [Wheeler, Sept. 15, C.R.]
Richard, s. Richard and Jemima, Feb. 27, 1730-1. [Wheeler, C.R.]

WHETNEE, Shadrah, s. Zacheus and Mary, Dec. 23, 1739. [Shadrach Whitney, C.R.]
Zaccheus, Mar. 14, 1739-40. [Zacheus Whitney, C.R.]

WHITAKER, Elizabeth, d. Samuel and Tabitha, Sept. 6, 1743.

WHITE, ———, twin s. Nathan and Dorcas, still born, July 22, 1789.

———, twin s. Nathan and Dorcas [July 26, 1789], a. 4 d.

———, inf. Caleb, fits, Sept. 13, 1799. C.R.

WHITFORD, Ann M., d. Seth and w., fever, Feb. 24, 1844, a. 5 y. 6 m.

Elizabeth, consumption, June 3, 1843, a. 20. [Elizabeth P., June 1, G.R.]

Ellen F., d. Hiram Webber and Bethiah, bowel complaint, Oct. 6, 1844, a. 4 m. 7 d.

WHITMOR (see Whitmore), John, s. John and Martha, Aug. 29, 1743. [Whitmore, C.R.] [Whitmore, a. 5 y. 10 m. 7 d., G.R.]

William, s. John and Martha, Sept. 11, 1743. [Whitmore, C.R.] [Whitmore, Sept. 11, 1745, a. 4 y. 5 m. 24 d., G.R.]

WHITMORE (see Whitmor), Ebenezar, s. John (Whitmoor) and Martha, Aug. 24, 1743. [Ebenezer, C.R.] [Ebenezer, Aug. 2, a. 2 y. 7 m. 23 d., G.R.]

John, Oct. 25, 1748, in 38th y.

John, s. John and Martha, Feb. 21, 1749-50. [a. 8 m. 8 d., G.R.]

Lucy, d. John and Martha, Feb. 16, 1749-50. [a. 4 y. 3 m. 8 d., G.R.]

Martha, d. John and Martha, Apr. 17, 1750. [a. 7 y. 6 m. 18 d., G.R.]

Mary, wid. John of Medford, d. John Lane and Susanna, Mar. 27, 1783, a. 96. G.R.

Susanna, d. Benjamin and Susanna Webber "late of Medford," grand d. John and Mary, Apr. 2, 1743, a. 15. G.R.

Susanna, d. John and Martha, Mar. 4, 1749-50. [a. 2 y. 7 m. 16 d., G.R.]

WHITNEY (see Whetnee).

WILLINGTON (see Wellington), Abijah of Waltham, "who came into town unwell, and dyed suddenly with dysentery," Oct. 1, 1803, a. 17. C.R.

WILLIS, Ellen, d. Josiah and Lydia, fever, Mar. 19, 1844, a. 4.

WILLSON (see Wilson), Amity, d. Amity, wid., Nov. 29, 1753. C.R.

David, Mr., Jan. 23, 1757.

Dolly, w. James, Feb. 21, 1841, a. 67 y. 11 d.

WILLSON, Ebenezer, Mar. 9, 1750-1. C.R.
James, June 24, 1753. C.R.
James, s. James and Dolley, Oct. 5, 1804, a. 3 y. 8 m. 14 d. [Wilson, ch. James Jr., "caught in a cider mill," a. 3 y. 9 m., C.R.]
James, July 14, 1819, a. 43 y. 8 m.
Jonathan, Capt., Apr. 19, 1775, in 41st y., "Killed in Concord= Fight." G.R.
Joseph Jr., Aug. 26, 1748. C.R.
Rebeckah, Mar. 27, 1789, a. 55 y. 10 m. 19 d.
Rhoda, d. Joseph, Dec. 17, 1753. C.R.
Samuel Jr., June 21, 1740. C.R.
Sarah, d. Amity, wid., Dec. 14, 1753. C.R.

WILSON (see Willson), Betsey, w. George, consumption, Aug. 26, 1846, a. 40.
Francis, m., s. James, consumption, July 25, 1845, a. 65.
James, s. James and Dolly, May 23, 1836, a. 31 y. 8 m. 26 d.
John, Lt., h. Rebecca, Feb. 1, 1734-5, in 84th y. [Willson, C.R.]
Jona[than], "with a complicated disorder," Sept. 27, 1797, a. "30 odd." [Sept. 25, in 35th y., G.R. C.R.]
———, ch. Thad[deu]s, May 19, 1803, a. 8 m., in Boston. C.R.

WOODWARD, Ellen Adelia, ch. George W. and Adelia B., Sept. 2, 1841, a. 3 w. G.R.
———, d. Geo[rge] W. and w., head complaint, Sept. 23, 1843, a. 1.

WOOLLEY, John, s. John and Mary, Oct. 4, 1754.
Jonathan, "by a fall from a Stone wall which killed him in a minutes time," July 25, 1766, in 61st y. [July 22, in 65th y., G.R.]
Samuel, Nov. 25, 1773, in 70th y. G.R.

WRIGHT, Dorcas, d. Joseph Page and w., Nov. 22, 1846, a. 71. [w. James, G.R.]
James, Dea., Dec. 24, 1818, a. 73. G.R.
James, Mar. 27, 1826, a. 51. G.R.
Margaret, d. James and Dorcas, May 10, 1832, a. 20. G.R.
Ruth, d. James and Ruth, Sept. 16, 1775, in 7th y. [Sept. 15, a. 7, G.R.]
Ruth, w. Dea. James, Jan. 6, 1830, a. 82. G.R.
Sally, d. James and Ruth, Sept. 2, 1775, in 4th y. [Sept. 1, a. 4, G.R.]
Timothy Page, s. James Jr. and Dorcas, Aug. 22, 1801. [Sept. 22, a. 20 m., G.R.]

WRIGHT, ———, ch. James Jr., still born, Oct. 17, 1797. C.R.
———, ch. James Jr., dysentery, Sept. 23, 1801, a. 20 m. C R.

WYLLIS (see Willis.)

WYMAN, Harriet, b. Woburn, d. Abel Pierce and w., fever, Nov. 13, 1843, a. 50. [wid. Samuel, Nov. 11, G.R.]
Samuel T., s. Sam[ue]l and Sarah, fever, Dec. 25, 1843, a. 1 y. 4 m.

NEGROES, ETC.

Cuff, "a negro child belonging to Mr Zacheus Whitney," Nov. 2, 1737. C.R.
Domine, "a Negro Boy who belonged to Mr John Lane Junr," Aug. 3, 1749. C.R.
Jack, a negro, old age, Apr. 15, 1800, a. abt. 80. C.R.
Peter, "a Revolutionary soldier, freed slave of Rev. Josiah Stearns, Epping, N.H., faithful hired servant of Rev. Samuel Stearns," ———, 1807. G.R.
Violet, colored, old age, June —, 1842, a. 100.

UNIDENTIFIED.

———, ———, "a child living with M^r. William Hartwell Junr.," Nov. 26, 1736. C.R.
———, ———, "a nurse child at W^m. Porters," May 18, 1804, a. 5 m. 2 [? d.]. C.R.

www.ingramcontent.com/pod-product-compliance
Lightning Source LLC
Chambersburg PA
CBHW030554080526
44585CB00012B/376